DYNAMIC
EXECUTION
FOR
EXECUTIVES

DYNAMIC EXECUTION FOR EXECUTIVES

Innovative Concepts And Tools For The Achievement Of Strategic Objectives

TOM SOMODI

INDIE BOOKS
INTERNATIONAL

DYNAMIC EXECUTION FOR EXECUTIVES
Innovative Concepts And Tools For The Achievement Of Strategic Objectives

© 2025 Tom Somodi

ISBN 13: 978-1-966168-09-6
Library of Congress Control Number: 2025904096

Designed by Melissa Farr, Back Porch Creative, LLC

Produced by CHANGE SCIENCE INSTITUTE, LLC (www.ChangeScienceInstitute.com)
in conjunction with
INDIE BOOKS INTERNATIONAL®, INC.
2511 WOODLANDS WAY
OCEANSIDE, CA 92054
www.indiebooksintl.com

Contents

Preface

There is a major dilemma engulfing executives. C-suite executives have been delegated the primary responsibility of guiding an organization in establishing direction, objectives, and strategic execution that produces continuous upward trends in performance. However, the knowledge, tools, and methodologies used to accomplish these responsibilities have a terrible record of success.

From small- to large-scale initiatives, on-time strategic execution resulting in desired objectives within the anticipated budget has unacceptably high failure rates.

Upon reflection, many executives will admit that the risk of failed strategic development and execution is a major source of ongoing concern and frustration—and rightfully so. My observations, along with a review of the literature on failure rates, substantiates the reality behind these concerns.

There are indications that 65 percent to 75 percent or more of strategic initiatives completely fail or fail to reach expectations.[1] This is not a new phenomenon; in fact, there are indications that unacceptable failure rates have not improved for more than twenty to thirty years.

If, as the saying goes, "insanity is doing the same thing over and over and expecting a different result," why do executives continue to use the same old concepts, tools, and methodologies that lead to such a high risk of failure?

However, the objective of this writing is not to analyze why the dilemma exists or continues to be perpetuated.

Instead, the objective is to provide executives with an introduction to Dynamic Execution.

Dynamic Execution represents new innovative concepts, tools, and methodologies that will significantly improve C-suite's ability to obtain the successful development and execution of strategic initiatives resulting in their desired objectives.

Thomas Somodi, 2025

1

Time Is An Enemy

Let's start with the premise that time is a major enemy of executives. Like you, over the years, I was bombarded with and accepted as rational, ridiculously long strategic initiative execution timelines. Timelines for major initiatives could stretch from twelve to eighteen to as many as twenty-four months.

The Dynamic Execution concepts, tools, and methodologies I am introducing here start with a head-on challenge to these unnecessary timelines.

Throughout the book I will establish opportunities available to reduce and manage these timelines. This book will explore in more detail the multiple aspects inherent within Dynamic Execution that directly address how, as executives, you can reduce the time of execution.

The following illustrations help reinforce what differentiates Dynamic Execution from the other historical methodologies.

These illustrations highlight how Dynamic Execution is a closed-loop, continuous capability to dynamically accelerate, decelerate, modify, and adjust priorities simultaneously across multiple strategic initiatives based on the monitoring and feedback of actual conditions.

This capability ultimately results in reduced execution times and increased executive success.

Illustration: A Year-End Organization-Wide Systems Upgrade

Dynamic Execution concepts, tools, and methodologies allowed an organization to fully implement and execute a year-end launch of a complete top-to-bottom, organization-wide, new enterprise system in four months.

This was accomplished even though the solution providers and other experts indicated it would take a minimum of twelve to eighteen months.

In addition, even though there was a complete transition to new engineering, sales, operations, and financial systems, there was little to no disruption in day-to-day operational activities or customer deliveries during or after the execution and launch.

Furthermore, the year-end financials were closed on time and had absolutely no audit journal entries.

Illustration: Preparations To Go Public

A company that decided to go public was told by all the experts it would take a year or more to meet all the necessary requirements.

Using Dynamic Execution, the actual timeline was reduced to six months.

Dynamic Execution not only continually monitors, analyzes, and controls a specific strategic initiative but supports the simultaneous dynamic scheduling and control of multiple strategic initiatives.

Dynamic Execution provides a clear understanding of the availability and timing of required resources. This creates an ability to dynamically determine what strategic initiatives are the most critical to focus on and when, using what resources, in a continuous flow that provides the desired objectives when actually needed, all while minimizing any disruptions to operations.

Illustration: Merging The Operations Of New Acquisitions And Expansions

The concepts, tools, and methodologies of Dynamic Execution provided the basis to consistently integrate the operations of major new acquisitions and expansions in six months or less.

My experience in rapidly growing organizations that included aggressive acquisition, expansion, and merger strategies was that there was a short window of opportunity to efficiently and effectively integrate and launch these new operations. As an executive, I found the efforts and likelihood of success become exponentially more difficult as the timeline extends past six months.

Dynamic Execution techniques provide the ability to avoid many of the challenges and failures associated with traditional approaches to the integration of new acquisitions and expansions.

Dynamic Execution

While you might see similarities to many traditional methodologies, you will come to realize that the incorporation of Dynamic Execution into your organization will be a major beneficial paradigm shift.

As depicted in the illustrations above, Dynamic Execution recognizes that execution time is an executive's worst enemy. Executives are often convinced that execution times are inherently long and complex. Traditional strategic execution concepts, methodologies, and approaches make it difficult for executives to understand, challenge, monitor, and control the execution efforts. Once approved, execution timelines can take on a life of their own. Dynamic Execution changes all of that by providing a clear and efficient pathway to understanding, monitoring, and controlling the execution of strategic initiatives that yield the objectives you strive for.

Dynamic Execution represents an integrated approach to the execution of critical organizational objectives. Dynamic Execution recognizes that it is executives who are in the best position to guide an organization by making sure strategic and operational efforts are integrated in a cohesive context throughout the entire organization.

I find the comparison of a person and their horse with that of a CEO and their organization a useful analogy: Both leading a horse and riding the horse are ways for you and the horse to go from point A to point B. In both cases, you are in control of the horse and are responsible for successfully leading the horse in the right direction.

However, there are obvious benefits to riding the horse versus just leading the horse. Both you and the horse are more directly a part of the process and find greater satisfaction in this involvement. You and the horse are acting as one, but you still have control of the direction. Going from point A to point B is faster and more efficient, resulting in less time-consuming effort on your part while obtaining superior success.

However, a horse can only reach maximum effectiveness if all four legs are not only healthy but operating together in a fully coordinated manner. I will describe the *whys* and *how* behind the organizational philosophy and structure used in Dynamic Execution that provide executives with the ability to lead their organization from an integrated perspective.

Dynamic Execution is a closed-loop management structure. It builds on an integrated organizational structure that includes a continuous bidirectional flow of critical events and information throughout the organization, going far beyond traditional operational reporting systems and dashboards. This closed-loop integrated structure is constantly focused on organizational objectives and initiatives within the context of day-to-day operational activities. It is intended to efficiently provide timely bidirectional information and feedback regarding organizational initiatives that are critical to executives.

Executives need to start thinking in terms of objective management instead of project management. Through this closed-loop integrated Dynamic Execution structure, executives and organizations not only obtain the ability to schedule and execute multiple objectives more efficiently and effectively, but to do so dynamically and simultaneously.

Dynamic Execution is based on science and actual experience. In this book, I will present a new pathway for executives and organizations to follow in their quest to successfully achieve organizational objectives.

It is a pathway based upon a recognition that all change follows a consistent set of laws, principles, and concepts. In other words, there is a science behind all change: change science. More importantly, change science can be leveraged to create concepts, tools, and methodologies that will efficiently and effectively improve the ability to fully accomplish organizational objectives.

No one would ever consider sending a rocket to the moon without relying on the science of physics. So why should we ignore the science of change when executing strategies that yield organizational objectives?

My last book—*The Science Of Change: Basics Behind Why Change Succeeds and Fails*, explored the science itself, whereas the focus of this book is not on the science but on how executives and organizations can use this science to improve their ability to successfully obtain organizational objectives.

You might be asking where these concepts were derived from and how the framework for Dynamic Execution was developed. The answer is from the study of change science and firsthand personal executive experience.

I have an interesting executive experience base with major responsibilities in both strategic execution and operations together with a strong background in finance.

I personally had ownership with executive roles in fourteen companies. Together with my additional executive positions in other major companies and my consulting roles, my experience covered everything from high-growth, high-tech products and services; traditional automotive and mainstream manufacturing, distribution, and services; software, internet, e-commerce, and telematics technologies; to business and executive consulting.

When asked what my job entailed, I would often say, "I am the person with the shovel and the broom who follows the parade."

This was because I had direct executive involvement in a significant number of start-ups, acquisitions, mergers, divestitures, greenfield expansions, and the execution of countless critical strategic execution initiatives. These activities were not only domestic but included China, Africa, Canada, Mexico, the UK, Japan, and the Caribbean.

I even orchestrated and executed a public offering with a market-cap increase approaching $900 million, providing a nine-times return to initial investors within three years.

What I will present is based upon all this direct executive experience dealing with the challenges of obtaining successful organizational change. Executive experience that, over the years, allowed me to develop an understanding of the science behind change and how the Dynamic Execution concepts, tools, and methodologies I am presenting here will significantly increase your ability to obtain the critical objectives you desire.

One might view the fact that an organization is operating in a dynamic environment as an obvious and simple concept.

However, I would point to Einstein's $E = mc^2$: simplistic yet significant in the ramifications it represents and often difficult to understand and apply.

At the obvious level, everyone knows that an organization operates in both an internally and externally dynamic environment. However, it is how executives deal with the challenges of these environmental dynamics that is so often misguided, overly simplified, or inadequate.

Through the Dynamic Execution concepts, tools, and methodologies I will be presenting, executives can improve their understanding and ability to address these dynamics. Executives will obtain a newfound, straightforward, innovative capability to successfully obtain their organizational objectives.

Timing Could Not Be Better: Artificial Intelligence (AI) And Other Emerging Trends

The timing for executives to embrace the new innovative concepts, tools, and methods I am presenting could not be better.

An executive's ability to succeed is only going to become even more challenging unless they start using more progressive and rapid responding approaches to the execution of critical objectives.

The dynamics executives are facing today are changing at a more rapid pace than ever before. The speed at which AI and other emerging trends are changing the landscape is almost beyond comprehension.

The great news is that Dynamic Execution and the other scientifically based concepts being provided here can instantaneously help executives in multiple ways. Foremost, they will assist executives in the effective and successful execution of objectives that incorporate these new technologies and trends. They will also assist executives in avoiding unnecessary risks surrounding such new technologies and other rapidly changing environmental dynamics.

Executives will come to recognize how these new innovative concepts and tools can be leveraged to enhance their capabilities by clearly determining and defining the *why, when, how*, and *by whom* associated with these new technologies.

Remember, the main overall objective of this book is to provide executives with new and superior concepts, tools, and techniques to accomplish their critical objectives through the innovative framework of Dynamic Execution.

2

Dynamic Execution Overview
American Football

In football, a team starts the season with the objective of winning the Super Bowl. They establish an overall strategy to accomplish this objective, taking into consideration such things as their existing and potential roster, what their schedule looks like, and the overall philosophy of the coaching and head office staff.

However, an interesting dynamic begins to take place. Instead of trying to drive this initial overall strategy into every game, they reassess and often tweak or even modify the strategy based on the actual conditions that exist for an upcoming game.

Conditions such as injuries, status of the opposing team, strengths and weaknesses at each position, and opposing team highlights are all taken into consideration. In turn, this reassessment leads to modifications to their overall strategy based upon these current existing conditions.

But it does not stop there. A continuous reassessment process, along with potential modifications, occurs throughout the game.

Feedback from the observations of the coaching staff and players, actual performance of the execution of specific plays on the field, and all sorts of other controllable and uncontrollable dynamics are constantly analyzed as the game progresses.

While the overall objectives of winning the game and progressing toward the Super Bowl are unchanged, the strategic execution is dynamic based on the monitoring and feedback of the actual conditions that exist at any point in time. The assumptions used to develop a specific strategy at the beginning of the season and before every game are closely monitored based on the actual conditions that exist.

This leads to the potential for dynamic adjustments to the strategy as the season and any given game progresses. These adjustments might be minor or major, but the management of the organization is open and receptive to the possibility that modification might, and probably will, be necessary.

I have just described a thirty-thousand-foot overview of the Dynamic Execution approach, which I will explain in detail.

Anyone in an executive position knows that the successful execution of strategies to obtain critical organizational objectives can be one of the most difficult but important challenges they confront.

Many of you might be thinking to yourself that, like the football example above, you run your organization dynamically.

Unfortunately, the reality is that these dynamics typically get lost when traditional strategic execution methodologies are employed.

The internet is full of statistics, which I am sure your personal experiences will probably support. Failure rates to execute strategies that yield an organization's desired objectives are unacceptably high. Plus, even when a desired objective is accomplished, there is a high probability that anticipated and acceptable timelines and costs are missed.

These outcomes are not limited to small or medium-sized organizations.

One only needs to look at the retailer Target's failed objective to penetrate the Canadian market as a prime example of a large organization's failure.[2] So, if large organizations with access to capital, highly trained technical staff, and major consulting expertise fail, what kinds of challenges do all the smaller organizations face?

As apparent in the football example, one must recognize that in any given game, one of the teams ultimately fails even though both teams are following the same dynamic process.

Therefore, there must be more to consider than just the dynamic monitoring and associated response to the actual conditions occurring during the game.

Other factors come into play, such as differences in the quality of players and staff, organizational structure and philosophy, and budgetary considerations between the teams. All of these factors affect the results of the game and the season.

Figure 2.1 indicates that the same is true of Dynamic Execution.

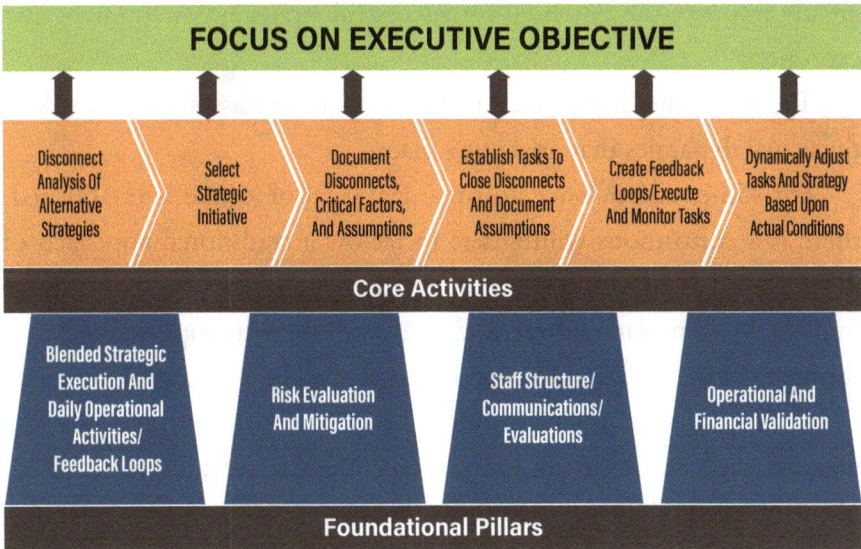

Figure 2.1

Dynamic Execution Overview

DYNAMIC EXECUTION

FOCUS ON EXECUTIVE OBJECTIVE

| Disconnect Analysis Of Alternative Strategies | Select Strategic Initiative | Document Disconnects, Critical Factors, And Assumptions | Establish Tasks To Close Disconnects And Document Assumptions | Create Feedback Loops/Execute And Monitor Tasks | Dynamically Adjust Tasks And Strategy Based Upon Actual Conditions |

Core Activities

| Blended Strategic Execution And Daily Operational Activities/ Feedback Loops | Risk Evaluation And Mitigation | Staff Structure/ Communications/ Evaluations | Operational And Financial Validation |

Foundational Pillars

Therefore, while the continuous dynamic monitoring, assessment, and adjustment of strategies and assumptions are core within Dynamic Execution, there are four other critical components in this executive management framework to explore: organizational philosophy and structure; the evaluation of risk; staff structure, staff communications, and staff evaluations; and incorporation of a continuous integrated operational and financial validation process.

I like to refer to these as the four pillars of Dynamic Execution supporting the core activities of Dynamic Execution, as found in the center of figure 2.1.

Key Aspects Of Dynamic Execution:
Paradigm Shift

To start, executives need to step out of the traditional box that experts and solution providers want to use.

Dynamic Execution represents concepts, tools, and methods that can greatly improve the potential for successful strategic development and execution.

The key is that there needs to be an ongoing reassessment based on the actual dynamics that are taking place.

For some reason, once an organizational objective is established, there is a continuous willingness to follow a traditional approach of putting a lot of effort into developing an execution strategy, selecting an implementation plan and methodology, and then attempting to slam it through the organization to what is expected to be a successful outcome.

On top of that, there is often a belief and commitment that the organization has the perfect upfront execution strategy, implementation plan, and methodology.

I believe this is based upon all the front-end effort expended, combined with unyielding confidence that a proven methodology has been selected and that help from the right group of experts has been solicited.

Therefore, this can lead to faith that if the organization is dedicated enough and pushed hard enough, it will have a successful result.

As I will present in this book, there needs to be a paradigm shift.

From an executive perspective, success should be focused on obtaining the important objectives they want to achieve as quickly as possible.

Success should not be determined by whether there is a successful ability to predict the future or select the best execution strategy, implementation plan, proven methodology, or experts.

I have found this real perspective often gets lost in the shuffle surrounding the process of strategic development and the focus on a specific selected implementation methodology.

Dynamic Execution represents this paradigm shift.

Dynamic Execution begins with an understanding that all day-to-day operational systems, methods, processes, and configurations in existence today are based upon the strategic initiatives executed in the past. Therefore, any modifications, adjustments, or changes to these operational activities are dependent on the future strategic initiatives that will be executed.

Consequently, executives and their organizations must realize that day-to-day operational activities and the execution of strategic initiatives should not be viewed as distinct efforts. Instead, the most effective organizational structure is an organization-wide continuous blending/integration of strategic execution activities with day-to-day operational activities.

There needs to be an ongoing reassessment structure within the organization of the selected strategy and strategic execution. This reassessment is based on the dynamics associated with the actual change in the conditions that exist at any point in time. The assumptions used to develop the strategy and execution plan need to be continuously monitored, assessed, and, when necessary, adjusted based on the actual conditions that exist.

The best way to support this continuous reassessment process is by using integrated top-to-bottom organizational feedback loops. These feedback loops represent feedback flowing down in the organization regarding strategic change drivers and assumptions and feedback flowing up in the organization regarding assumptions to use and the status of actual conditions.

In addition, to support this blended strategic execution/operations organizational structure, executives need to embrace an innovative approach to human resource management. This approach represents a new HR evaluation, communication, and staff integration methodology—a methodology that improves the executive's ability to make HR decisions within a dynamic environment, significantly supports the improved integration and involvement of the organization's workforce into C-suite initiatives, and provides executives with an easy-to-use tool to quickly determine and monitor the strengths, weaknesses, and exposures associated with an organization's human resources.

When taken together, a major benefit is that the time associated with a strategic execution is no longer represented by some fixed, demanding timeline. Instead, strategic execution becomes a continuous integrated process with timing becoming adaptive. This allows for a more responsive execution and a high potential for a much shorter execution timeline, concepts that we are going to explore in much more detail.

Another major aspect of Dynamic Execution centers around the assessment, monitoring, and control of risk. It starts with a recognition of the change science environmental override principle. Environmental override describes how all requirements for any given process/strategy must be available within the environment in which the process/strategy will be executed or that process will fail to execute.

Consequently, it does not matter if you have selected a proven process/strategy; it will not be executed without the availability of all the necessary requirements. If there are missing requirements, then an *implementation* must take place with the goal of establishing the availability of any missing process requirements. However, this implementation will be occurring in a world of complexity where perpetual change is constantly taking place.

The same complexity makes it literally impossible to reliably predict up front the absolute best strategy. Therefore, all this perpetual change represents a risk that the implementation will fail to obtain the necessary process requirements and, thus, the ability to obtain the successful execution of the selected strategy.

Once again, the length of time to execute adds to this challenge. This is because the complexity/perpetual change (and, therefore, risk) increases as the interval of time it takes to obtain all the necessary strategy requirements increases.

To address these challenges, Dynamic Execution introduces the concept and tool of disconnect analysis. This tool determines and analyzes the disconnects between the requirements of any given process/strategy and the actual environmental conditions that exist.

Disconnect analysis determines the context and exactly what requirements are missing for the selected strategy. It also becomes an effective tool to assess any alternative strategies under consideration. For example, let us say that the passing strategy used by a football team relies heavily on a given offensive lineman who, unfortunately, becomes injured. The coach will do an unconscious quick discount analysis of the alternatives of using the running back as an additional pass blocker or shifting to a more aggressive running game. If the running back is known to be a strong blocking back, then there is a match between the strategy requirement and the required condition, and the coach continues to rely on the passing game.

It must also be recognized that all decisions in strategic development and execution are based upon some level of assumptions. Thus, the accuracy of these assumptions inherently represents an additional potential risk. Therefore, besides defining disconnects between actual existing conditions and strategy requirements, a disconnect analysis must document any critical assumptions that are being relied upon.

Clearly documenting the critical assumptions used in the selected strategy and implementation creates a strong basis for their communication and monitoring using feedback loops. This, in turn, allows the executives and organization to quickly address and react to any issues that arise from any inaccurate or missing critical assumptions or conditions.

I cannot stress this concept enough: the determination, documentation, monitoring, and ultimately control of critical assumptions provide a major tool for executives and organizations to reduce risk and increase their potential for successful results!

Incorporated within Dynamic Execution is a recognition that not all risks are created equal. Some risks are more controllable than others, and the significance and probability of risks can differ considerably. Therefore, an organizational focus on an ongoing analysis and the ability to eliminate or mitigate certain risks can greatly increase the potential to obtain the desired objectives.

Suppose you have a controllable risk factor. In that case, that risk factor should be eliminated, provided the significance of the risk factor justifies the time, effort, and cost of elimination. However, if the risk factor is uncontrollable, then, when possible, that risk factor should be mitigated, provided the significance of the risk factor justifies the time, effort, and cost of mitigation.

Finally, Dynamic Execution challenges operations and finance to create an integrated structure that is dynamically responsive to the analysis of the existing changing conditions and assumptions.

Finance needs to have analysis and modeling capability that can quickly and immediately analyze the financial impacts associated with the operational feedback received from the monitoring of assumptions and actual conditions. This analysis is not intended to be a replacement for traditional operations or financial reporting, which tends to have a delay in availability. Instead, it is intended to be incorporated into the monitoring, control, and feedback system, which is much more time-sensitive and near-term.

In conclusion, embedded within this overview of the Dynamic Execution methodology is the fact that it represents an integrated closed-loop perpetual system.

Therefore, the overall risk is reduced through this integrated closed-loop strategic execution/operations system. This significantly increases the ability to obtain the successful accomplishment of executive objectives.

PART I

Dynamic Execution Foundational Pillar

Blended Organization Structure And Feedback Loops

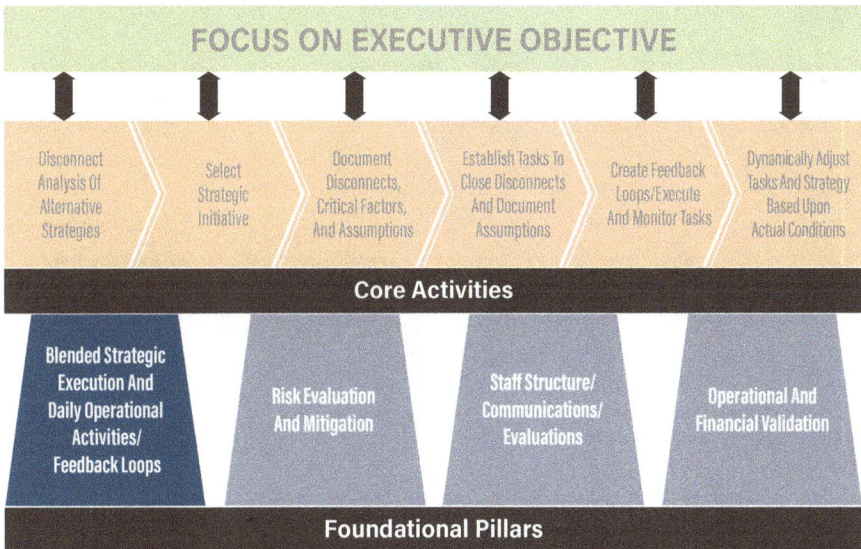

FOCUS ON EXECUTIVE OBJECTIVE

| Disconnect Analysis Of Alternative Strategies | Select Strategic Initiative | Document Disconnects, Critical Factors, And Assumptions | Establish Tasks To Close Disconnects And Document Assumptions | Create Feedback Loops/Execute And Monitor Tasks | Dynamically Adjust Tasks And Strategy Based Upon Actual Conditions |

Core Activities

| Blended Strategic Execution And Daily Operational Activities/ Feedback Loops | Risk Evaluation And Mitigation | Staff Structure/ Communications/ Evaluations | Operational And Financial Validation |

Foundational Pillars

Chapters 3, 4, and 5 explore an organizational structure with the blending of strategic execution with operations activities and the use of feedback loops.

Dynamic Execution Foundational Pillar

Blended Orchestration Structures And Feedback Loops

Blended Organization Structure And Feedback Loops

Many years ago, I had a discussion with a CEO about the frustration that existed regarding the inefficiency of certain operational processes in the organization. I asked how these processes came to be in the first place and was told they were the result of a major strategic initiative launched by a prior executive.

At the time, my training and experience were traditional in a context where organizations from an operational perspective were functionally and departmentally compartmentalized. Strategic initiatives were considered special projects that required implementations of new objectives that are driven down and infused into the organization.

It was not uncommon for operations to view the execution of these strategic initiatives as major disrupters to their day-to-day responsibilities and activities. While matrix organization structures requiring staff to have dual responsibility and reporting between functional and project responsibilities existed, they tended to be only in very large organizations. This left most smaller to medium and large organizations organized in a functional context.

However, even these matrix-structured organizations delineated the execution of strategic initiatives as projects versus daily operational activities.

So, both organizational structures, and in my opinion, all the alternative and derivative structures and project execution approaches and methodologies that I have been exposed to, adhere to this same distinct daily operational versus strategic execution activity mindset presented in figure 3.1.

Figure 3.1

Strategic Activities

Change activities (projects) required in response to internal influences, perceived opportunities, and reaction to external influences

Traditional Perspective
Treat As Two Distinct Sets Of Activities

Operational Activities

Required day-to-day activities executed to support an organization's ongoing operational existence

At the time of my discussions with the CEO, I recognized that from a holistic point of view, the execution of the strategic initiatives required changes in the operations of the organization.

I followed the traditional approach of strategic development and used an implementation plan to drive the necessary changes into the operations to execute those strategic initiatives.

I recognized that there was risk associated with a successful outcome and used consultants and service provider experts to assist in the execution of the strategic initiative. However, I struggled with this traditional type of approach, and even back then, the literature was full of studies indicating excessively high strategic execution failure rates.

Much of the rationale behind these failure rates, though, focused on a lack of management commitment, a rationale I really found somewhat crazy. After all, it was the executives who had already committed to the execution of the project, some of the best staff in the organization, major financial resources, and even hired some of the best consultants for these projects.

For some reason, this exercise with this CEO made me realize I needed to more closely explore this strategic-to-operational interrelationship.

Interestingly, around that same time, my neighbor came to me for advice about their desire to start a new business.

They started by asking basic strategic questions. "How should I price my services? What are your thoughts on the best way to market my services? Should I start by automating my processes or manually executing my processes?" The list of strategic questions went on.

Here, we discussed a potential new organization with no current operations at all. The starting point was strictly the development and execution of strategies that, if successfully executed, would result in the operations of a functioning organization.

This led me to recognize that there was a direct interrelationship and set of dynamics that existed between day-to-day operational activities and strategic execution activities. And, even though conceptually simplistic, this interrelationship represented a platform that could be used to create an organizational structure that could yield major opportunities for executive and organizational success in obtaining their desired objectives.

The interrelationship, as depicted in figure 3.2 is that all of the processes and capabilities currently used in day-to-day operations (daily activity) are a result of historically executed/implemented strategic change (executed strategic initiatives).

It is through the implementation of new strategic change driven by new objectives that the systems, methods, and procedures used in day-to-day operations will be created and modified.

Figure 3.2

Actual Relationship Between Strategic Execution And Operations

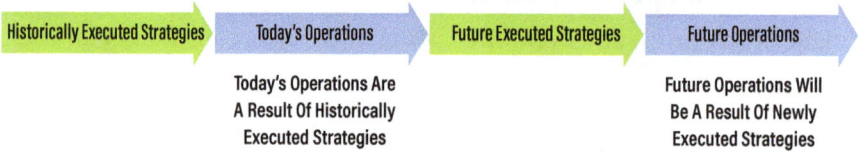

Historically Executed Strategies	Today's Operations	Future Executed Strategies	Future Operations
	Today's Operations Are A Result Of Historically Executed Strategies		Future Operations Will Be A Result Of Newly Executed Strategies

Obviously, there is a tremendous amount of information and guidance available about strategic development, strategic execution, and how to effectively execute an organization's day-to-day operations. However, it is the lack of recognition of the actual interrelationship and dynamics between strategic execution and operational activities where existing information, guidance, and understanding are lacking and even inaccurately represented.

Therefore, it is important that executives realize there is a strategic basis to any of the operational systems, methods, and procedures executed in daily operations.

Even staff who decide, with no formal approval, to change the way they perform a task are executing a self-developed strategy they believe will create an operating procedure that, for whatever reason, is better than the one formally established.

In other words, all changes to daily operational systems, methods, and procedures can have a strategic impact on the organization, even if they do not have an "approved strategic initiative" label attached to them. Large or small, these changes are de facto strategic changes and, in many cases, have major impacts on success or failure within the organization.

It is critical that these highly interrelated dynamics are recognized and capabilities are established to monitor, control, and, most of all, leverage these dynamics. Herein rests a premise that exists within Dynamic Execution:

Organizations exist to provide services and products. To do this, they require an operational structure. However, this operational structure must be created, which is accomplished through the execution of change via strategic initiatives. The guidance, establishment, and direction of this change/strategy can be controlled or uncontrolled, but in the ideal, it comes from a controlled focus on established executive objectives. Therefore, for an organization to have continuous improvement, there must be a continuous execution of successful objectives through the execution of strategic initiatives.

The bottom line is, as highlighted in Figure 3.3, there is a direct interrelationship between day-to-day operational activities and strategic activities. The main focus of Dynamic Execution is to make sure continuous improvement and change occur within a controlled context and with a focus on the successful accomplishment of executive objectives.

Figure 3.3

Continuous Improvement Through Controlled Objective Focused Strategic Execution

Historically Executed Strategies → Today's Operations → Future Executed Strategies → Future Operations

Today's Operations Are A Result Of Historically Executed Strategies

Future Operations Will Be A Result Of Newly Executed Strategies

Change/Time Continuum →

Continuous Improvement - Controlled Strategic Execution And Operational Changes Focused On Accomplishment Of Established Executive Objectives

Many might think that controlling, much less leveraging, these dynamics down to the individual level is unrealistic. However, by starting with this recognition of what the actual strategic execution-to-operations relationship looks like, we can now explore how executives can accomplish this.

Paradigm Shift: A Blended Strategic Execution And Operations Organization Structure

While there are all sorts of discussions regarding the need for executives to maintain solid strategic direction or create efficient, well-running daily operations, these discussions tend to be discrete and limited in focus. They fail to really develop a context that allows executives an ability to fully integrate the dynamics between all these strategic and operational events. In fact, it is more common than not that strategic execution is viewed by operations as nothing but a disrupter, and executives struggle to determine how to obtain successful change.

Unfortunately, it is the lack of understanding of the dynamics described here that creates a propensity to perpetuate the execution of methodologies and approaches that have high degrees of failure.

As already pointed out, there are indications that as many as 65 percent to 75 percent or more of strategic initiatives completely fail or fail to fully reach expectations.[3] In addition, even those that succeed regularly exceed their expected launch dates and/or are over budget.

Unfortunately, the tendency is for executives to continue to rely and focus on traditional strategic-to-operational execution methods. These methods develop implementation plans that are then driven down into the organization.

As shown in figure 3.4, these plans tend to follow strict implementation and project management guidelines that are inflexible, act as a major disrupter, can extend the time required to implement, and that can create conflicts in organizational priorities, daily operations, and among staff.

Figure 3.4

Traditional Strategic To Operational Implementation
Implementation Plans Are Created And Driven Down Into The Organization

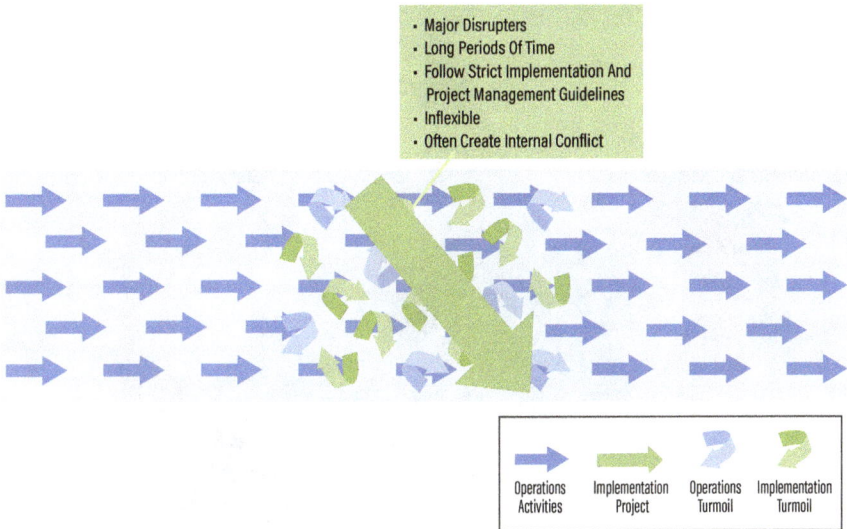

- Major Disrupters
- Long Periods Of Time
- Follow Strict Implementation And Project Management Guidelines
- Inflexible
- Often Create Internal Conflict

| Operations Activities | Implementation Project | Operations Turmoil | Implementation Turmoil |

The goal of executives must shift to an organizational structure that combines strategic initiative activities with day-to-day operational activities.

There needs to be a paradigm shift and usage of new innovative concepts and tools. Through this paradigm shift, executives will not only be able to start to blend strategic execution with day-to-day operations but will experience a significant improvement in overall organizational success.

Feedback Loops

Figure 3.5 introduces the creation of organization-wide feedback loops as a part of the paradigm shift. These feedback loops represent feedback flowing down into the organization regarding strategic change drivers and assumptions, as well as feedback flowing up in the organization regarding assumptions to use and the status of actual conditions.

Figure 3.5
Paradigm Shift
Creation Of Feedback Loops

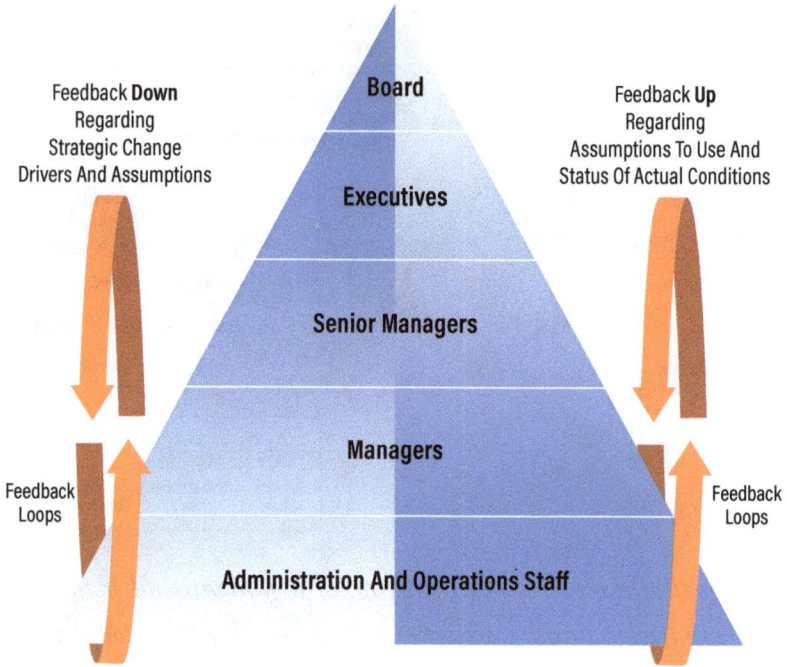

Feedback **Down** Regarding Strategic Change Drivers And Assumptions

Feedback **Up** Regarding Assumptions To Use And Status Of Actual Conditions

Board

Executives

Senior Managers

Managers

Administration And Operations Staff

Feedback Loops

Feedback Loops

As shown in figure 3.6, incorporating feedback loops will help blur the lines between strategic initiatives and day-to-day operations.

More importantly, they will turn the execution of strategic initiatives into a continuous integrated process. The continuous nature of this integrated process not only generates faster results, but is less disruptive, reduces conflict, is dynamic, and provides an ability to support actual condition-to-assumption monitoring. These are all critical topics that we will explore in more detail.

Figure 3.6

Paradigm Shift Away From
Traditional Implementation

Blending Of Strategic Initiatives With Day-To-Day Operations

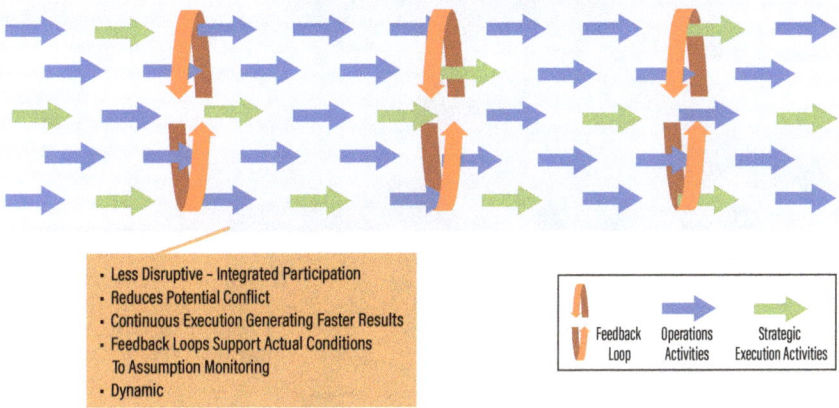

- Less Disruptive - Integrated Participation
- Reduces Potential Conflict
- Continuous Execution Generating Faster Results
- Feedback Loops Support Actual Conditions
  To Assumption Monitoring
- Dynamic

Feedback Loop | Operations Activities | Strategic Execution Activities

Another way to depict the difference between traditional strategic execution and the paradigm shift is to think of day-to-day operations as a stream of flowing water. Traditional implementations of strategic change are like inserting a board into the middle of the stream. The board becomes a major disrupter to the stream of day-to-day operations, with water hitting the board and being forced to flow around it and backing up behind it.

Now, envision a structure where that strategic implementation is like dropping a block of ice into the stream of water. The ice becomes integrated with the flowing water, gradually melting and blending into the operations stream, creating circular currents of information feedback loops. This feedback then helps determine the structure, context, and location of the next block of ice that is dropped into the stream: a continuous process of the blending of strategic initiatives with day-to-day operations.

Strong feedback loops provide a basis that can be used to efficiently determine, understand, and monitor the underlying strategic conditions and assumptions. They are like a GPS system. Feedback loops can instantaneously tell the organization where they are, what is happening relative to strategic initiatives, and what direction to take, all of which greatly increase the potential for success.

4

Continuous Improvement For The Launch Of A Blended Organization Structure

Early on in my career, I made an interesting observation about organizational hierarchy based on executive parking. As shown in figure 4.1, the entrance was dead center into the office building, which was only a short distance from a long sidewalk in front of management parking.

Figure 4.1

Organizational Hierarchy And Executive Parking

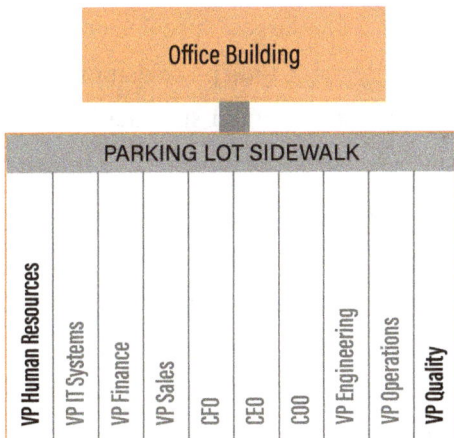

The interesting thing was not that the chief executives were the nearest to the entrance, but that the management of quality control and human resources were the furthest away.

This observation gained increased meaning to me later when I realized how many Japanese organizations, especially in the automotive and electronics industries, became dominant players through a focus on—guess what—quality and human resource management. Many would contend that this dominance continues to this day with, for example, Toyota.

William Edwards Deming

I always found the story of William Edwards Deming fascinating. Here was someone whose concepts (such as continuous improvement) were initially shunned by the United States automotive industry only to be embraced by the Japanese auto industry.[4]

In the end, the adoption of Deming's philosophies on quality and human resource management would propel Japanese automotive makers such as Toyota into world dominance. These philosophies were further reinforced through personal experience when I was an executive at a large automotive supplier.

When I started with the company, it was the third-largest supplier in their product category. The largest supplier was multiple times larger.

Then, an interesting dynamic took place that propelled our organization to become the largest, most dominant supplier in the industry.

When the push came from the automotive industry for suppliers to embrace a focus on quality, continuous improvement, and just-in-time capabilities, our executive leadership had the foresight to fully embrace these requirements while our competitors pushed back and dragged their feet.

This led me to ask a basic question that I will now ask you as the current executives of your organizations: If concepts such as continuous improvement through the monitoring of actual-to-required results and driving down responsibility, staff involvement, and empowerment throughout the organization work in operations, why wouldn't these concepts also be beneficial to use in strategic execution to obtain desired objectives?

Many organizations recognize the significance behind the concept of continuous improvements from an operational perspective while totally missing the application as it pertains to strategic execution.

Therein lies the basis for a blended strategic execution and operations organizational structure with feedback loops!

Superior organizational performance will result in a continuous improvement structure for successfully executing strategic objectives.

In addition, the accomplishment of executive objectives through the integrated ongoing commitment of staffing resources under a blended strategic execution/operations organization structure will automatically generate efficiencies and additional capacities, leading to the creation of the future staffing necessary to perpetually support this blended structure.

In other words, over time, this structure represents a system that self-generates the ability to provide the staffing resources necessary to support the continuous execution of future objectives.

Executives commit a portion of existing staff resources through the blending of strategic execution responsibilities with daily operational responsibilities. These committed resources execute objectives that generate additional staffing capacity. For example, if an objective generates additional revenues, the profitability from those added revenues provides the ability to support additional staffing. Or if an objective produces improved operational efficiencies, those efficiencies yield additional available capacity from existing staff.

This new capacity can then support the execution of the next set of executive objectives, ultimately making this a self-generating, self-supporting, and perpetual system.

When continuous improvement is applied to strategic execution in a blended strategic/operations organization structure, the benefits derived from the successful accomplishment of objectives will yield the creation and perpetuation of available staff resources.

Risk: Staff Participation And Commitment

Lack of staff participation and commitment to strategic development and execution can represent a major risk to an organization's ability to obtain their desired objectives.

Obviously, the level of time committed by an individual to participation in strategic initiative development and execution versus day-to-day operations can vary significantly. It can be heavily dependent on the position and responsibilities any given staff member has within the organization. However, the expectation of top-to-bottom staff participation and commitment is a realistic goal.

The structure created through a blending of strategic execution with operations is accomplished through the proper level of incorporation of strategic development and execution into each position within the organization. This creates the potential for a seamless structure with little to no differentiation at the positional or individual level between strategic initiative and operational responsibilities. In other words, the goal is to make an appropriate level of strategic participation and commitment a routine part of each individual's responsibilities.

In chapters 8 through 11, I will describe an innovative human resource management methodology that explains how to incorporate and support this blended structure all the way down to the individual staff level. Ongoing participation and commitment are then obtained and reinforced through feedback loops.

Once again, this downward communication of strategic initiative information and feedback upward of critical information regarding strategic initiatives should become a seamless part of each individual's day-to-day activities. This structure allows the level and context of this feedback activity to vary depending on the position, timing, and requirements of the strategic activity taking place.

The creation of this comprehensive top-to-bottom blended structure will greatly enhance the C-suite's ability to reduce the risk associated with staff participation and commitment.

Incorporating A Blended Strategic Execution/ Operations Structure And Feedback Loops

To start with, executives must realize that a full-out ongoing commitment to this type of organizational structure is required. It represents an incorporation as a part of executive philosophy and desired culture.

This is not something that can be tested out for a while and then fully launched later. As executives, you must recognize the following realities that exist:

- Historically, unless specifically assigned to a strategic execution role like project manager, the organization and staff are inherently wired to focus on daily operational responsibilities.
- Historically, strategic initiatives have been viewed as one-off projects with a start and completion. Strategic execution has not been recognized as a continuous process leading to ongoing improvements in day-to-day operations and performance.
- Historically, time requirements and necessary commitments by staff to execute strategic initiatives are already consuming individual and organizational human resources. However, as discussed in detail later in this chapter, this existing consumption of staff resources for strategic execution is done in a context that is (a) generally poorly defined and delineated, (b) extremely inefficient, and, given the failure rates, (c) ineffective.

Therefore, from a consumption of staff resources perspective, as executives, you are already either inefficiently deriving the strategic objectives you desire, or you are not even bothering to attempt to obtain the necessary critical objectives you are looking for because of a perceived lack of, and/or disruption of, available resources.

In other words, committing your organization to a blended strategic execution/operations structure with feedback loops will, at worst, represent a net zero additional use of staff resources.

However, in reality, Dynamic Execution will represent significant benefits in the efficient use of staff resources and a continuous ability to successfully derive an increase in the number of successful strategic objectives you can accomplish.

Steps To Incorporate Strategic Initiative Execution Into Staff Daily Activities

I have found that the acceptance and participation of the staff grow significantly when these concepts are presented in the context of a learning experience, an opportunity for increased involvement and empowerment in organizational change, and a feeling of accomplishment through their participation in the efforts.

Under this context, the following training should be initiated.

Explain the relationship among strategic change, daily operations, and the need for continuous improvement. The need for continuous improvement through the execution of new strategies and change is not a complicated concept. In most cases, there will already be a major segment of staff familiar with the concept of continuous improvement.

Explain disconnect analysis and how this will require soliciting their input and participation (we will explore disconnect analysis in detail in chapter 6).

Explain how the communication channels will work. In chapters 8 through 11, I will delve deeper into staff communications and innovative concepts in human resource management, structure, evaluations, and assessments. The key focus here is an explanation of the need for feedback loops: the bidirectional flow of information with feedback flowing down into the organization regarding strategic change drivers and assumptions and feedback flowing up in the organization regarding assumptions to use and the status of actual conditions, and the need for their participation in the monitoring and analysis of actual versus assumed conditions.

Explain how staff will receive feedback regarding progress and accomplishments.

Explain how an individual's contribution and performance in strategic execution activities will be recognized and incorporated into their personal assessment (see chapter 11 on staff evaluations and HR resource analysis capabilities).

Benefits Of A Continuously Executing Blended Organization Structure

I hope it is obvious that a blended organization structure, together with other facets of the Dynamic Execution system, provides executives with a solid, structured, and consistent way of communicating and aligning their desired organizational objectives with their staff. It is not haphazard and fluctuating from project to project, but is a laser-focused set of innovative concepts and methods.

Another benefit is that a blended organization encourages engagement. It promotes and supports the individual's desire for participation and accomplishment, provides individuals with an understanding of the significance of their participation, and represents true staff empowerment.

In addition, a blended organization structure creates a continuous and Dynamic Execution of objectives. It provides dedicated and continuous allocation of required resources; actual versus assumed condition monitoring, analysis, and control; and simultaneous multi-objective execution. It supports dynamic scheduling across multiple strategic executions based upon changing priorities, actual availability of resources, and other actual environmental dynamics.

An often missed but powerful aspect of the blended organizational structure with feedback loops is the efficiency and superiority of the staff training associated with the operational launch of the objectives.

Staff participation is now incorporated from the beginning of the process, providing direct exposure not only to the *why* but also to what the critical factors are and how the accomplishment of the new objective will actually work. This provides a tremendous opportunity to efficiently integrate training into the execution process itself, avoiding back end efforts—faster launch at a lower cost!

This represents a system that is self-generating and self-supporting. As detailed above, when continuous improvement is applied to strategic execution in a blended strategic/operations organization structure, the benefits derived from the successful accomplishment of objectives will yield the creation of perpetuating available staff resources.

5

Guidance For Blending Strategic And Operations Staffing Responsibilities

Energy/Effort/Capability Hump Considerations

Illustration: An organization determined that a major upgrade in the enterprise system was required to support future growth. They selected a popular vendor's hardware and enterprise software system after an extensive review of alternative packages in the marketplace.

The organization also decided to utilize the selected vendor's implementation methodology, along with their recommended system configuration and implementation consulting expertise. It was estimated that the implementation would take between twelve and eighteen months to complete. Under the recommendation and direction of the vendor's consultants, the organization committed staff to the project on an as-needed basis.

I was brought in because after more than two years, the initiative was over budget, behind schedule, and failing to provide any sort of realistic benefit with no clear completion date in sight.

There was a total miscalculation of the level of human resource commitment, both in time and capability. The organization had failed to recognize that given the existing workloads of the staff and the continually fluctuating demands of the implementation, the staff would become overwhelmed. This created not only issues with the implementation, but also with the organization's ability to satisfy day-to-day customer service requirements and staff commitment to the project.

In addition, while the consultants could provide the expertise relative to the system they were providing, the implementation still required internal expertise that just did not exist.

From a traditional strategic-execution project-methodology perspective, what this organization was experiencing is what I refer to as the energy/effort/capability hump theory disconnect.

I refer to it as a hump theory because, from a traditional perspective, the execution of a strategic initiative has a level of staff time, effort, and capability associated with it to be successful.

Given that day-to-day operations also require an ongoing level of staff time, effort, and capability, the traditional implementation methodology being used creates a "theoretical hump" in the amount of required staff resources.

Figure 5.1 depicts how this hump represents the amount of additional required time versus the amount of actual available time during the execution of the initiative.

If, after taking into consideration the demands of day-to-day operations, there is insufficient available time, effort, and capability to support the execution of the strategic initiative, a disconnect is created.

Figure 5.1

Traditional Methodologies

Energy/Effort/Capability Hump Theory

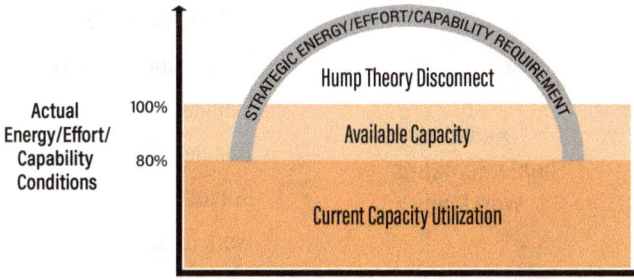

As already discussed, executives intuitively recognize that the project implementation plan represents a demand for staff resources. They also accept that this staffing requirement will need to be executed in conjunction with day-to-day operational activities.

However, their focus tends to be on the demand for staff on a project-by-project basis, not as an ongoing requirement.

In addition, while executive presentations will usually outline some sort of staffing requirements analysis, a true understanding of the dynamics associated with staffing is most often missing.

As shown in figure 5.2, the reality in a traditional strategic execution context is that the staff requirement shortfalls for any given project must be compensated for with some sort of mix between six alternatives.

More importantly, these dynamics are not some global organizational set of requirements but are requirements that, more often than not, cross-departmental/functional lines all the way down to the individual level.

Figure 5.2

Traditional Methodologies

Alternatives For Addressing Hump Disconnect

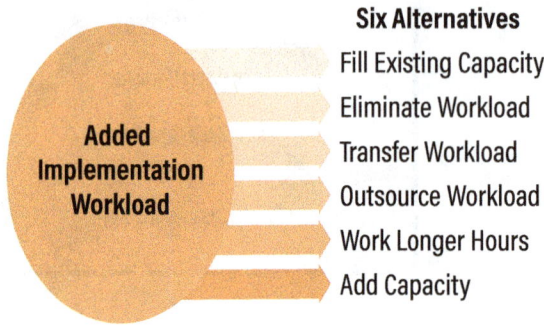

Six Alternatives

**Added
Implementation
Workload**

Fill Existing Capacity

Eliminate Workload

Transfer Workload

Outsource Workload

Work Longer Hours

Add Capacity

If executives take a step back and look at these alternatives closely, they should see some immediate potential issues:

Has there really been an adequate analysis of available existing capacity (i.e., the true magnitude of the disconnect between required and actual)? And, if so, is that available capacity within the context of individuals who have the actual required capability to execute the implementation?

What workload will be eliminated? Will the eliminated workload need to be backfilled later? What are the ramifications of daily operational activities related to the eliminated workload?

What exact workload can be transferred? Do the internal resources receiving the workload have existing capacity, or will the transfer just create a ripple effect within the organization? If it is an operational activity, do the internal resources receiving the workload have the existing knowledge and capability to backfill the requirements? If not, how long will it take to train them, and what are the risks if they fail to perform? If it is project implementation activities, do the internal resources receiving the workload have sufficient knowledge and understanding of the organization's actual operations and requirements?

Which exact workload can be outsourced? If it is an operational activity, do the outsourced resources have the existing knowledge and capability to backfill the requirements? If not, how long will it take to train them, and what are the risks if they fail to perform? If it is project implementation activities, do the outsourced resources have sufficient knowledge and understanding of the organization's actual operations and requirements? Or are they going to make decisions or implement approaches that instead force the organization into a structure that more readily complies with the canned systems being implemented?

If the solution includes working longer hours, how many hours, who will do that, and how has this been determined? What is the cost of these added hours? Will these hours be effective or will there be inefficiencies due to scheduling of time requirements based on availability of consulting resources? What will be the impact on staff morale and commitment? How often can these demands be placed on staff?

Finally, if we added capacity, how long would it take to train those additional resources, and what would the costs of associated inefficiencies and exposure to errors in execution be?

With regard to my efforts relative to the strategic execution in the illustration, the good news was that I was able to assist the organization in completing the execution of the strategic initiative in less than six months. This was accomplished by determining the essential requirements and performing a comprehensive resource-to-disconnect analysis.

Note that in chapter 15 we will develop a deeper explanation of the concepts behind a resource-to-disconnect analysis.

The key here is that by developing a more comprehensive understanding of the dynamics and capabilities that existed within the organization, I was able to more realistically incorporate the strategic execution with day-to-day operational staff commitments.

Executive Guidelines: Strategic Execution And Operational Responsibilities

It must be recognized that while it is obvious that the execution of a strategic initiative requires staff time, effort, and capability, that is not the challenge for executives.

The challenge for executives is in the quantification, monitoring, control, and blending of these requirements with the ongoing day-to-day requirements of operations.

Receiving a detailed implementation plan that stretches over months, if not years, is, at best, of limited value—especially to executives and especially if the focus is more on the successful implementation of a specific software or operational system. Again, executive success is when their desired objective is accomplished in a timely manner. It is not when a selected methodology is implemented but with limited to no accomplishment of the desired objective.

The real primary value is a clear understanding of all the disconnects that exist and what it will take to eliminate those disconnects. Therefore, the commitments of staff time, effort, and capability can be directly associated with specific disconnects. This provides executives with a straightforward, easy-to-understand picture of the "what will it take and why." In addition, it provides the organization with a significantly superior structure for managing the exact timing of these resources and an improved ability for coordination with day-to-day operational requirements.

The ability to reach executive objectives in a timely and efficient manner is even further magnified when this resource-to-disconnect structure is combined with an organization that blends strategic initiatives with day-to-day operations. The blending and feedback loops inherently provide the capability to manage, monitor, and control any energy/effort/capability hump theory disconnects that might exist.

Finally, as we will see in chapter 7 regarding the challenges associated with "when not if," the resource-to-disconnect analysis is a critical element in supporting a strategic execution methodology that includes the ability to set dynamic priorities and support dynamic scheduling.

Existing Strategic Execution Resource Commitments Are More Than You Might Think

Your first reaction when looking at the guidelines I am about to discuss is, "No way." "No way the amount of staff resources consumed by strategic executions should represent such a large commitment of staff time."

The simple answer is that this reaction is due to a lack of recognition of the number of existing activities that actually represent strategic execution versus day-to-day operational activities.

Remember, all day-to-day operational systems, processes, requirements, and activities are a direct result of historically executed strategies. Therefore, any activity, even ongoing activity, that expands, modifies, adjusts, or resolves conflict within these operational systems, processes, requirements, and activities represents an already existing commitment of strategic execution resources.

Some of these strategic events might be short versus long in duration, temporary versus permanent, focused on revenue versus cost, or even reactive versus planned, but they are all nonetheless strategic activities that consume resources. That is why, when you review the guidelines that follow, you will see that the focus on strategic execution responsibilities increases as you progress up an organization's hierarchy.

It is important for executives to recognize that by properly recognizing certain activities as strategic executions versus operational activities, you have established a more accurate required relationship to a desired objective.

In other words, by recognizing the direct relationship between a strategy and objectives, you have created a necessary link to your requirement to obtain a successful objective or objectives. Therefore, the decisions and executions associated with these strategies will now be in the context of supporting the accomplishment of a successful objective.

An activity/responsibility should be considered strategic if it affects the structure of daily operational systems, processes, requirements, and activities and/or requires the consideration of any ramifications related to established executive/organizational objectives.

In contrast, operational activities/responsibilities are all the daily organizational activities executed using these established operational systems, processes, requirements, procedures, and activities to provide services and products to the marketplace.

In my context, operational activities are considered broad-based and include everything from marketing and sales, service offering or product support, service/product production and delivery, post-sale support, or any other daily activities necessary to provide the service and product offerings associated with the ongoing existence of the organization.

Warning: What I am attempting to stress here is that, as executives, we often underestimate or fail to recognize the significance and potential impacts related to the number of strategic activities actually taking place daily within our organizations.

However, the key point is not if you agree or disagree with what I am defining as strategic versus operational. Nor is it meant to have you assess how accurate you are at recognizing strategic versus operational activities.

Instead, the intent is for you as executives to recognize that there is more strategic activity already occurring within the organization than is actually recognized. Especially at positions from the Sr. Manager/Director level and up within the organization. Therefore, moving to a blended/operations organization structure does not automatically represent an increase in staffing but a reallocation and more efficient concentrated focus of existing resources on strategic activities to obtain your objectives.

Therefore, this blended strategic/operations organizational structure will help you as an executive. You can create a staff-wide understanding of what strategic activities are and how important they are not just to the organization but to the way they perform their daily activities. You also form a structure that focuses these activities on accomplishing specific objectives and on using established objectives as guidelines for use during their decision-making versus haphazard, unfocused decisions that are often made to address spur-of-the-moment issues.

You also provide an environment that fosters staff participation in strategic activities through an understanding of the importance of accepting the blending of these responsibilities with their daily operational activities, as well as an environment that provides staff with a sense of involvement, accomplishment, growth, and empowerment that stretches beyond their day-to-day operational responsibilities.

A blended organizational structure will provide executives not only the ability to more effectively and efficiently utilize the time already being consumed on strategic activities within the organization, but will significantly improve the ability to cost-effectively obtain more objectives in less time and with greater staff participation.

Guidelines For Assignment Of Strategic Execution Responsibilities

Given the diversity in structures, staffing, strategic activities, and external/internal environmental considerations among organizations, there are no hard-and-fast rules or configurations for the balancing of strategic activity responsibilities with daily operational activities. Therefore, the best approach is to focus on the assignment of responsibilities for strategic activities versus some sort of analytical approach, such as an assignment of specific time commitments.

In other words, it is best to indicate to your staff that, "Here are your specific responsibilities when it comes to the execution of strategic activities," versus saying, "I expect you to spend X number of hours or X percent of your time on strategic execution."

While I do not want to downplay the amount of effort that can be associated with each of these responsibilities, when viewed in this context, the responsibilities are really very straightforward, easy to understand, and uncomplicated to communicate. These strategic responsibilities can be described under five main categories that are incorporated into the tables in figures 5.3 and 5.4.

Figure 5.3

Goals/Objectives/Strategic Execution Responsibility Assignments

Large Organization Strategic Responsibilities						
Activity	Board	C-Suite	Executives	Directors	Managers	Operations Staff
External And Internal Environment Analysis						
Analysis Of External Environment And Opportunities	X	X	X			
Analysis Of Internal Environment And Opportunities	X	X	X			
Feedback On Internal Environment					X	X
Feedback On Potential Internal And External Opportunities				X	X	
Vision / Goals / Objectives						
Oversight, Reality Check, And Assistance With Vision/Goals/Objectives	X					
Creation Of Vision/Goals/Objectives		X	X			
Feedback On Goals And Objectives			X	X	X	
Strategy Selection						
Oversight And Selection Sign Off Of Potential Strategies/Solutions		X	X			
Analysis, Evaluation, And Selection Of Potential Strategies/Solutions			X	X	X	
Risk Analysis Associated With Potential Strategies/Solutions				X	X	
Feedback On Potential Strategies And Risks						X

Activity	Board	C-Suite	Executives	Directors	Managers	Operations Staff
Execution Plans For Selected Strategy						
Sign Off Of Execution Plans For Selected Strategies		X				
Oversight And Sign Off Of Execution Plans For Selected Strategies			X			
Analysis And Creation Of Execution Plans For Selected Strategies Including Monitoring, Control, And Feedback Points				X	X	
Feedback On Analysis And Execution Plans For Selected Strategies						X
Execution Of Selected Strategies						
Oversight Of Dynamic Scheduling And Execution Of Plan/Tasks			X			
Dynamic Scheduling Of Execution Plans				X	X	X
Execution Of Assigned Required Strategic-Execution Tasks				X	X	X
Oversight Of Critical Factor And Risk Monitoring/Control/Feedback			X			
Assumption And Critical Factor Monitoring/Control/Feedback				X	X	X
Resolution Analysis And Recommendations For Detected Assumption And Critical Factor Issues (Including Potential Modifications And Revisions To Selected Strategies And Execution Plans)				X	X	
Risk Monitoring/Control/Feedback				X	X	X
Resolution Analysis And Recommendations For Detected Strategic-Execution Risk Events (Including Potential Modifications And Revisions To Selected Strategies And Execution Plans)				X	X	
Sign Off Of Resolutions For Detected Issues Exposed From Assumption, Critical Factor, And Risk Monitoring/Control/Feedback		X	X			

Figure 5.4

Goals/Objectives/Strategic Execution Responsibility Assignments

Small And Medium Organization Strategic Responsibilities					
Activity	Advisory Board	Owner And Executives	Sr. Managers	Managers	Operations Staff
External And Internal Environment Analysis					
Analysis Of External Environment And Opportunities	X	X			
Analysis Of Internal Environment And Opportunities		X	X	X	
Feedback On Internal Environment					X
Feedback On Potential Internal And External Opportunities				X	X
Vision / Goals / Objectives					
Oversight, Reality Check, And Assistance With Vision/Goals/Objectives	X				
Creation Of Vision/Goals/Objectives		X			
Feedback On Goals And Objectives			X	X	X
Strategy Selection					
Oversight And Selection Sign Off Of Potential Strategies/Solutions		X			
Analysis, Evaluation, And Selection Of Potential Strategies/Solutions			X	X	
Risk Analysis Associated With Potential Strategies/Solutions			X	X	
Feedback On Potential Strategies And Risks					X
Execution Plans For Selected Strategy					
Oversight And Sign Off Of Execution Plans For Selected Strategies		X			
Analysis And Creation Of Execution Plans For Selected Strategies Including Monitoring, Control, And Feedback Points			X	X	
Feedback On Analysis And Execution Plans For Selected Strategies					X

Activity	Advisory Board	Owner And Executives	Sr. Managers	Managers	Operations Staff
Execution Of Selected Strategies					
Oversight Of Dynamic Scheduling And Execution Of Plan/Tasks		X			
Dynamic Scheduling Of Execution Plans			X	X	X
Execution Of Assigned Required Strategic-Execution Tasks			X	X	X
Oversight Of Critical Factor And Risk Monitoring/Control/ Feedback		X			
Assumption And Critical Factor Monitoring/Control/Feedback			X	X	X
Resolution Analysis And Recommendations For Detected Assumption And Critical Factor Issues (Including Potential Modifications And Revisions To Selected Strategies And Execution Plans)			X	X	
Risk Monitoring/Control/Feedback			X	X	X
Resolution Analysis And Recommendations For Detected Strategic-Execution Risk Events (Including Potential Modifications And Revisions To Selected Strategies And Execution Plans)			X	X	
Sign Off Of Resolutions For Detected Issues Exposed From Assumption, Critical Factor, And Risk Monitoring/Control/ Feedback		X			

External and internal environment analysis: First, in order to develop meaningful and effective goals and objectives, executives and the organization must have a continuous grasp of external and internal environmental conditions and dynamics.

Vision/goals/objectives: This understanding of the external and internal conditions and dynamics will become the basis for executives' establishment of organizational goals and objectives.

Strategy selection: These goals and objectives, in turn, drive the activities necessary to determine potential strategies and solutions to accomplish these goals and objectives, leading to the selection and signoff of a specific strategy or set of strategies.

Execution plans for selected strategies: Attention can then be focused on the analysis and requirements for the creation of an actual execution plan for the selected strategies.

Execution of selected strategies: Finally, the release of these execution plans drives the strategic execution activities necessary to accomplish the objectives while simultaneously and continuously monitoring for possible issues. If issues are uncovered, resolutions are determined that can be signed off on and acted upon. These execution activities include dynamic scheduling of execution plans; execution of assigned required tasks; assumption, critical factor, and risk monitoring/control/feedback; and resolution analysis, recommendations, and sign-off for detected assumption, critical factor, and risk issues (including potential modifications and revisions to selected strategies and execution plans).

Figures 5.3 and 5.4 depict these assignments within the context of an organizational staffing structure. These can be used to further assist executives in the creation of a blended strategic/operations organization structure using assigned responsibilities.

Figure 5.3 represents assignments for a large organization, while figure 5.4 represents these assignments in a small to medium-sized organization.

It should be noted that besides providing a guideline to use when assigning strategic activity responsibilities, there are other important characteristics that are highlighted within these figures. A close examination highlights how the feedback loop infrastructure I have described plays an integral role as an efficient information and data communications vehicle between the levels of the organizational hierarchy.

From the analysis of external and internal environmental conditions and dynamics for the creation of goals and objectives down through the actual execution of required tasks and monitoring of actual conditions, there is a well-defined top-to-bottom integrated hierarchical flow in responsibilities supported by the continuous bidirectional flow of critical information and data through the use of organization-wide feedback loops.

In addition, figures 5.3 and 5.4, together with figure 5.5, clearly indicate that it is middle management such as Directors/Sr. Managers and Junior/VP Level Executives that are at the center of the development and oversight of the execution of strategies along with the blending of the strategic and operational activities for the accomplishment of the objectives. Lower management and operational staff are focused on the actual execution of the tasks required to accomplish the strategic activities, along with providing the monitoring and feedback activities required to monitor, analyze, and communicate the risks and actual versus assumed critical conditions.

Therefore, in the ideal, C-suite/Senior Executive management should be primarily focused on the strategic activities of understanding internal and external conditions, the development of objectives based upon the understanding of those dynamics and conditions, and the continuous oversight and sign-off associated with the creation, execution, condition monitoring, issue resolution, and possible adjustments to the strategic initiatives required to accomplish their objectives.

This represents an extremely efficient, effective, and well-defined structure for executive involvement, monitoring, and control of strategic execution activities within the organization.

Analytical Perspective

I realize that there are those that want some sort of analytical quantitative perspective on what the allocation between strategic execution activities and operational activities looks like. And I also agree that there can be value associated with such a quantitative perspective.

For example, from a budgeting and staffing availability perspective, a macro understanding of the requirement of resources for each staffing level within the organization can help put a reality check on what commitments and priorities can be set on strategic execution activities. Therefore, the following is some guidance regarding such an analysis.

Figure 5.5 provides guidance for some of the workable macro averages that I have employed. However, the reality is that actual time commitments can/will/should fluctuate based on specific individuals and the balancing of actual operational and strategic conditions and demands at any point in time.

As executives, figure 5.5 helps you from a global perspective to visualize, quantify, conceptualize, and plan up front a certain amount of your staffing resources that will be committed to strategic execution activities.

For example, if you have twelve managers and assume an average of 15 percent of their time during the year will be consumed by strategic execution activities, you should expect that the full-time equivalency of around 1.8 managers will be utilized during the year. This is based upon 15 percent of 12 managers = 1.8 full-time equivalents.

Figure 5.6 takes the analysis one step further across a broader portion of the organization and includes not only an estimation of full-time equivalent staff but also an estimate of actual hours associated with strategic versus operational activities.

Figure 5.5

Average Strategic Versus Operational Activity Allocations

	Focus On Strategic Activities	Focus On Day-To-Day Operations
Board Of Directors	100%	0%
C-Suite	85% – 90%	10% – 15%
Executives	75% – 80%	20% – 25%
Directors/Sr. Managers	40% – 60%	40% – 60%
Managers	10% – 15%	85% – 90%
Operations Staff	5% – 10%	90% – 95%

Figure 5.6

Macro Modeling Of Commitments To Blended Strategic Execution And Operation Activities

Modeling Of Organization-Wide Strategic Versus Operation Activity								
Hierarchical Position	Number Of Total Staff	Average Percent Committed To Strategic Execution Activities	Average Percent Committed To Daily Operational Activities	Assumed Gross Available Annual Hours Per Staff	Average Total Staff Hours Committed To Strategic Execution Activities	Full-Time Staff Equivalency Committed To Strategic Execution Activities	Average TOTAL Staff Hours Committed To Daily Operational Activities	Full-Time Staff Equivalency Committed To Daily Operational Activities
Executives	4	80%	20%	2,080	6,656	3.2	1,664	0.8
Directors/Sr. Managers	6	50%	50%	2,080	6,240	3.0	6,240	3.0
Managers	15	15%	85%	2,080	4,680	2.3	26,520	12.7
Operations Staff	100	7%	93%	2,080	14,560	7.0	193,440	93.0
Total Organization	125				32,136	15.5	227,864	109.5
Percent Of Total Organizational Commitment					12.4%	12.4%	87.6%	87.6%

While this sort of exercise can be beneficial for high-level analysis and planning purposes, I still highly caution you against trying to assign responsibility for strategic execution responsibilities/activities using specific time commitments such as X number of hours or X percent of a department or individual's time. The reason is that, within the Dynamic Execution system, there are concepts, tools, and procedures we will introduce later in this book that provide much more flexibility and responsiveness to the actual conditions that exist at any point in time. These include resource-to-disconnect analysis and dynamic scheduling, as found in chapter 15.

Once again, the key is that staff recognize they have an ongoing fluctuating dual set of responsibilities and time requirements for both operational and strategic activities.

While this type of analysis may be helpful in selective analytical situations, I would suggest just assigning staff-specific responsibilities like those presented in the tables in figures 5.3 and 5.4.

In this context, managers should work with their staff to determine how to balance the workload and address any concerns or suggestions they might have. This allows the staff to adjust the workloads automatically according to responsibility.

Since, at any point in time, your staff is closest to the actual demands that exist, it is in the organization's best interest that the staff is empowered whenever possible to control the execution of both responsibilities.

Finally, as I already pointed out, as executives, it is important to recognize that, in reality, a level of staff commitment is already dedicated to strategic execution activities. Unfortunately, the level and effectiveness of the utilization of this staffing is generally not adequately understood or quantified, making control and management of these efforts difficult, ultimately leading to inefficiency, missed opportunities, and failed strategic executions.

Dynamic Execution addresses these shortfalls by providing superior strategic execution concepts, tools, and methods for the accomplishment of executive objectives. It provides a built-in level of resources available for strategic execution but within a dynamic context. This significantly improves management and control over these efforts, leading to increased success in obtaining more of your objectives more efficiently and in a shorter period of time.

PART II

Dynamic Execution Foundational Pillar

Risk Evaluation And Mitigation

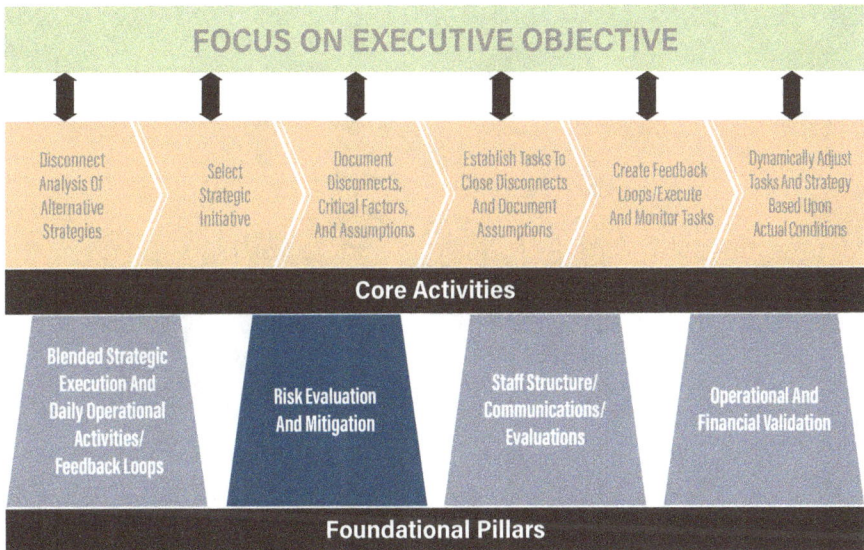

FOCUS ON EXECUTIVE OBJECTIVE

| Disconnect Analysis Of Alternative Strategies | Select Strategic Initiative | Document Disconnects, Critical Factors, And Assumptions | Establish Tasks To Close Disconnects And Document Assumptions | Create Feedback Loops/Execute And Monitor Tasks | Dynamically Adjust Tasks And Strategy Based Upon Actual Conditions |

Core Activities

| Blended Strategic Execution And Daily Operational Activities/ Feedback Loops | Risk Evaluation And Mitigation | Staff Structure/ Communications/ Evaluations | Operational And Financial Validation |

Foundational Pillars

Chapters 6 and 7 provide a deep-dive
executive perspective into risk.

6

Risk Basics For Executives
Texas Hold'em

Nothing Is Certain Except Uncertainty

While I am not a big gambler, I do enjoy watching the dynamics associated with the final table at a good Texas Hold'em tournament.

Here, you have individuals with a keen understanding of statistics and probability, a deep historical base of experience, and the ability to directly see and read their competition.

However, the ability of any particular player to win is still never a given because even with all this expertise, they do not know what the next card will be that is turned or what hand their competitor really has.

Therefore, it is amazing that so much of the success of an executive's strategic development and execution efforts is predicated on the ability to predict the future when having a consistently reliable method to do so does not exist.

In fact, there are studies that indicate the ability to influence the future because of wealth (like the largest stack of chips at the table) will more likely lead to increased success than any sort of actual methodology for predicting the future.

However, as borne out in Target's 2013 to 2015 failures at entering the Canadian market, even wealth (or the largest stack of chips) can have its limitations for successful strategic execution.[5]

But there was more to learn from the dynamics at the Texas Hold'em table that helped me reinforce what I learned after many years of C-suite experience in strategic development and execution.

Closely watching the players, you realize they reassess the dynamics of the game and, therefore, their next move after every new card appears or a competitor's bet. The key is that they do not start a tournament or a hand with a given strategy and just follow it through to the end, no matter what is actually happening during the progression of the game. Instead, there is a constant reassessment of their strategies based on the progression of the actual known conditions.

Therefore, there is a better way for executives to develop and execute strategic change than repeating the same old approaches that, in reality, have very poor success rates. Once again, there are indications that as many as 65 percent to 75 percent of strategic initiatives completely fail or fail to reach expectations.[6]

The good news is that if executives step out of the traditional box that experts and solution providers want to use, there are concepts, tools, and methods that can greatly improve the potential for successful strategic development and execution.

The key is to focus on the understanding, calculation, and control of risk versus just trying to predict future events, outcomes, and conditions accurately. There needs to be an ongoing reassessment based on the actual dynamics that are taking place.

For some reason, once an executive/organizational objective is established, there is a continuous willingness to follow a traditional approach of putting a lot of effort into developing an execution strategy, selecting an implementation plan and methodology, and then attempting to slam it through the organization to what is expected to be a successful outcome.

On top of that, there is often a belief and commitment that the organization has the perfect up-front execution strategy, implementation plan, and methodology.

I believe this is based upon all the front-end effort expended, often combined with an unyielding confidence a proven methodology has been selected and that help from the right group of experts has been solicited. Therefore, there is the belief that if the organization is dedicated enough and pushes hard enough, it will have a successful result.

Unfortunately, executives are presented with a sufficient amount of evidence of previous success, together with ongoing promotion of these traditional approaches, to convince them that this is the best alternative available.

However, there are, in fact, innovative concepts, tools, and techniques that can be utilized versus these traditional approaches.

From an executive's perspective, success should focus on obtaining the important objectives that the executive wants to attain as quickly as possible. It should not be whether there was a successful ability to predict the future or select the best execution strategy, implementation plan, proven methodology, or experts.

I have often found this real perspective gets lost in the shuffle surrounding the process of strategic development and the focus on a specific chosen implementation methodology.

To stay focused on the objective, we need to start with a discussion and understanding of some basic risks.

Environmental Override: Risk

The first thing to recognize is that all change/strategic execution requires the execution of a process.

Every process has a certain set of requirements for it to execute successfully. I can have a gasoline engine but need gasoline available for it to operate (a process requirement).

Therefore, all requirements for any given process must be available within the environment the process will execute in or that process will fail to execute.

In change science, we refer to this as the environmental override principle.

Consequently, it does not matter if you have selected a proven process/strategy; that process/strategy will not be executed without the availability of all the necessary requirements.

Example: Proven Process

In my presentations, I sometimes like to show the group a process that has been proven. For example, figure 6.1 represents the proven process of a pump to obtain the objective of a specifically shaped inflated balloon.

Figure 6.1

Example Of A Proven Process

I ask someone to come up and use a deflated balloon connected to a pump; they are instructed to see how fast they can inflate the balloon to accomplish the objective. It usually takes twenty to thirty seconds.

I then ask a second individual to come up and, with a second pump and deflated balloon, see if they could reach the objective faster than the first individual. Unbeknown to them, this balloon has some unseen holes in it. So, when they attempt to blow the balloon up, it fails to inflate or, at some point, bursts.

In other words, the conditions associated with the balloon do not match the requirements of the process.

So, I give them a third pump with a deflated balloon, and this time, they are able to inflate the balloon, but the balloon is a different shape from the shape of the balloon indicated in the objective.

The activities of the first individual substantiated that the process in figure 6.1, in fact, was able to reach the objective in their environment. However, the attempt of the second individual highlights that a successful strategic execution needs more than just a proven process.

All the conditions that exist in any given environment must include all the requirements necessary for that proven process to work. If they do not, even a proven process will fail. The pinholes in the balloon represent a lack of a necessary condition.

The third attempt reflects the potential danger executives and organizations face when a strategy/process/implementation is successful, but the results do not fully meet the real desired objective. The inflated balloon was a different shape than the balloon in figure 6.1, and therefore, the true objective was not really obtained.

Executives must never lose sight that it is not whether a strategy/process/implementation is successfully obtained if it does not result in your desired objective.

Having a successfully reached objective must always remain an executive's focus!

Implementations Versus Strategies And Processes

The terminology of strategy, process, and implementation can often get confusing.

A strategy is a plan, tactic, approach, or methodology to obtain an objective.

A process is a sequence of specific steps, activities, and actions that, when executed, achieve a specific result. A process has a set of requirements (process factors) associated with it that must be present for that process to work.

So, what then is an implementation?

An implementation is a series of actions (which ironically can include the execution of various necessary processes) required to ensure the conditions in a given environment match all of the necessary process requirements to execute that process.

Figure 6.2 is an example showing that if a given process has missing requirements or there are conditions that hinder the execution of the process, then an implementation must take place with the goal of establishing the availability of any missing process requirements or the elimination of any impediments.

Example: Implementation

Figure 6.2

Implementations = Creation Of Required Conditions

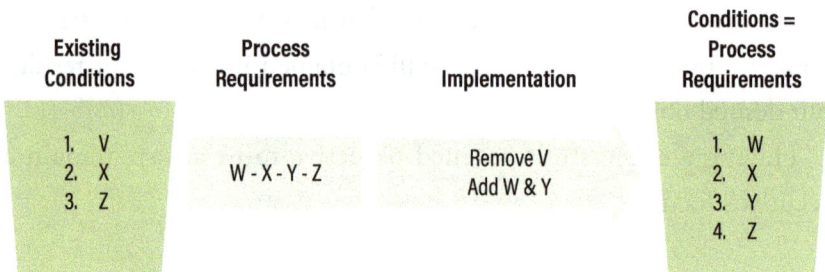

Existing Conditions	Process Requirements	Implementation	Conditions = Process Requirements
1. V 2. X 3. Z	W - X - Y - Z	Remove V Add W & Y	1. W 2. X 3. Y 4. Z

Caution Regarding Traditional Approaches

During my career, it was not uncommon to run into the following type of dialogue and logic regarding having a proven process and proven implementation capabilities. Solution provider: "My process is proven; my implementation methodology is proven; my project management capabilities are proven; pay now; given everything is proven, any failure is on you."

Actual Result = Historically Unacceptable Failure Rates

There are absolutely situations in which third-party solution sets, expertise, and methodologies are not only beneficial but necessary. However, executives must keep in mind that these solutions and services are available in the context of a profit model. That means broad-based generic solution offerings and time-based charging for services are advantageous and, therefore, the norm.

Therefore, executives need to recognize that it is within this context that things like (a) timelines and (b) required implementation efforts associated with these solution sets are being established.

Under traditional approaches, it is very common that solution sets/ strategies are selected based on having the "functionality" needed to provide the capabilities necessary to accomplish an organizational objective.

Consider, for example, the functionality found in a certain vendor's software system, a piece of equipment, operational configuration, or staffing structure. Since it is determined that the selected solution set has the required functionality, the focus becomes the implementation of that specific functionality and the associated selected solution.

This focus is often reinforced by the hype that the selected solution set is proven in the marketplace, and therefore, if you do not obtain the functionality, you have done something wrong.

Unfortunately, these traditional approaches are missing some realities. The conditions in every organization are different. Therefore, there can be significant differences in the required implementations. In turn, this leads to different levels of effort, potential issues, and appropriateness issues for the accomplishment of the objective. This is the real reason, in most cases, that proven functionality and implementation methodologies fail. It is not that the organization did anything wrong; it is because there was not a clear recognition of the actual efforts that existed, leading to unexpected challenges and/or the need for extended execution timelines.

In future discussions in this book, I will continue to explore how Dynamic Execution focuses up front on the actual disconnects, functionality trade-offs, assumptions, and tasks required to make a specific strategy work in your specific organization. Therefore, the organization obtains a superior indication of not just the effort and potential issues but of the overall fit and risks associated with any given solution or strategy.

Once again, executive focus must remain on the accomplishment of the objective and not whether a specific solution or implementation plan is successful.

Fortunately, there is a tool executives can utilize within the organization to help assess and address these risks.

Figure 6.3 presents how, within Dynamic Execution, disconnect analysis is just that tool.

Figure 6.3

Dynamic Execution Disconnect Analysis

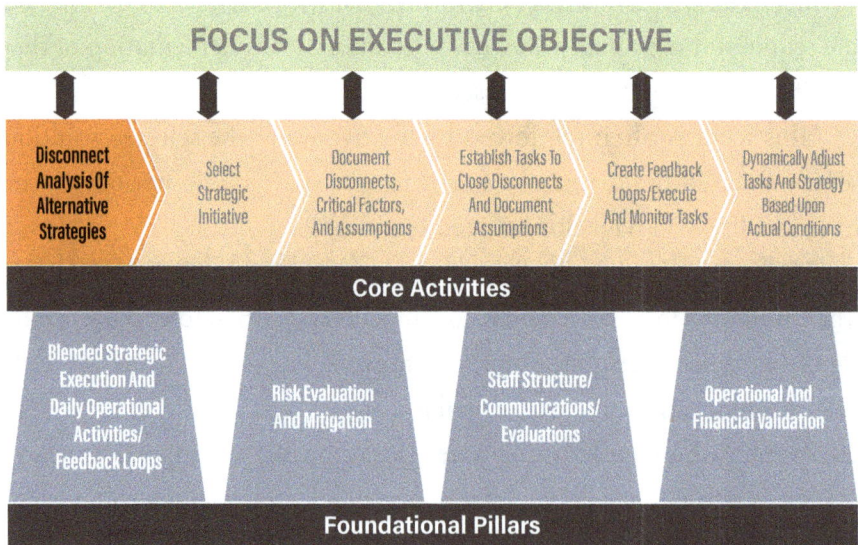

Disconnect analysis is a tool that determines and analyzes the disconnects between the requirements of any given process/strategy and the actual conditions that exist in the environment where that process/strategy will be executed (your specific organization).

Obviously, if all the necessary requirements already exist in an environment, the strategy will already be able to be executed, and the executive's objective will be obtained. No implementation to provide missing requirements will be necessary.

However, if there are missing requirements, then a disconnect analysis can determine the context and exactly what requirements are missing.

In addition, it is important to recognize that each potential alternative strategy under consideration for use to obtain a desired objective will have its own set of disconnects. That means that each alternative strategy will also have its own implementation requirements.

Given that each set of disconnects and implementation plans will be unique, there will exist an opportunity to at least estimate the time, effort, and resources required to execute each alternative implementation plan and strategy.

Therefore, disconnect analysis becomes an incredibly powerful tool for not only assessing the scope, disconnects, efforts, and time requirements for any given potential strategy but also for comparing and selecting among alternative potential strategies.

Disconnect analysis is an easy-to-understand, straightforward way to begin to assess the risk associated with strategic development, selection, and execution. It also becomes a great starting point for the use of the core Dynamic Execution system.

To successfully use disconnect analysis, an organization must not only determine all the critical requirements of a strategy but also determine the actual conditions that exist within the environment where the strategy will be executed. The missing or conflicting conditions represent the disconnects.

Therefore, comprehensive top-to-bottom integrated feedback loops become an excellent way to increase the ability to accurately determine requirements, actual conditions, and disconnects.

Feedback loops provide information flowing down the organization regarding strategic change drivers and assumptions being made at the upper levels of the organization. This, in turn, provides an opportunity to receive feedback flowing up in the organization regarding the critiquing of assumptions to use and providing the status of the actual conditions that exist.

In the end, executives have created a more comprehensive organization-wide capability to receive the input necessary to perform an effective disconnect analysis.

Example: Disconnect Analysis

In my presentations, I sometimes like to show the group the following picture of new, unmounted automotive tires shown in figure 6.4. I explain that each tire represents a separate and unique organization.

Then I ask the question, "By looking at these tires, who could tell me how much air is required in each tire?" Of course, it is almost impossible to know for sure how much air is needed in each tire just by looking at them.

Figure 6.4

Example – Assume Each Tire Represents A Different Organization

I then present the picture in figure 6.5 showing the use of a tire gauge.

Figure 6.5

Disconnect Analysis Is Like Using A Tire Gauge

I explain that disconnect analysis is like using a tire gauge. It analyzes actual conditions versus process requirements, defines exact conditions missing for your specific situation, and provides an up-front definition of specific efforts, actions, and resources.

Assumptions/Predictions/ Disconnect Analysis: Risk

Given the discussion above on predictions, some might be questioning how I differentiate between predictions and assumptions.

An assumption is to have an expectation of something with some, little, or no proof. It can be in the context of the current or future.

As an example, a current assumption would be, "I assume the product is upstairs." A future assumption would be, "I assume that the product will be delivered on time."

A prediction is to have an expectation of a future event or outcome generally based upon data, knowledge, or experience, but not always. It is a best or informed guess of the current or future.

For example, a current prediction is, "The product has historically been located upstairs, so that is where the product will be." A future prediction would be, "Based upon a historical on-time delivery rate of 90 percent, I predict the product will be delivered on time."

A prediction can be considered an assumption focused on an event or condition generally based upon some sort of informed or analytical basis. Therefore, it is easier for executive purposes to just use the single-term assumption, recognizing that it is in the broader context that includes predictions.

However, the important concept to focus on is not the definition of assumptions versus predictions. Instead, in both cases, the focus must be on the risk associated with these assumptions/predictions and how to determine, monitor, and control that risk.

There is a reality that exists that is often missed, ignored, or viewed as a weakness.

All decisions are based on some level of assumptions.

While these assumptions can have a wide range in the variable of probability and, therefore, the importance of consideration, assumptions, in fact, represent a potential risk in strategic development, selection, and execution.

Therefore, besides defining disconnects between actual existing conditions and strategy requirements, a disconnect analysis must document any critical assumptions being used in the process.

For example, a critical assumption might be that there will be a consistent level of sales during the time frame of the implementation. Therefore, a major deviation in sales represents a potential risk and the monitoring of this assumption as it relates to the strategic initiative would be valuable.

Clearly documenting the critical assumptions used in the selected strategy and implementation creates a strong basis for communication and monitoring through the use of feedback loops. This, in turn, allows executives and the organization to quickly address and react to any issues that arise from any inaccurate or missing critical assumptions or conditions.

I cannot stress this concept enough: The determination, documentation, monitoring, and ultimately control of critical assumptions provide a major tool for executives to reduce risk and increase their potential for successful results!

The Science: A New Understanding, Concepts, And Tools

We start with a basic question: but why?

Why is it so difficult to predict and establish accurate assumptions that lead executives to the selection, implementation, and execution of effective strategies?

The simple, and what many will say obvious, answer is that all this activity is occurring in a world of complexity where perpetual change is constantly taking place—a complexity that makes it literally impossible to predict the future consistently and reliably.

This perpetual change and complexity represent a risk to an organization's ability to obtain a successful execution of the selected process/strategy. This risk is the real challenge for executives.

However, as basic and obvious as this all is, there is actually a scientific basis that explains it. When understood, this scientific basis can assist us in developing concepts, strategies, and tools that will help executives significantly improve their ability to obtain the objectives they are striving for.

Change Science Chain Of Events Principle And Perpetual Change Risk

The change science chain of events principle and law of perpetual change can be summarized as follows:

- Processes executing now = new conditions
- New conditions support the execution of new processes
- This chain of events is continuously repeating
- Thereby creating perpetual change

In other words, there are processes executing this very second that create a new set of conditions, which in turn will support all the necessary requirements for the execution of a new set of processes.

So, the new set of conditions triggers the execution of these new processes, which, once again, create a new set of conditions.

This chain of events is self-perpetuating and will continue indefinitely, creating perpetual change.

But our scientific understanding does not end there.

Change/Time Continuum Principle And Law Of Simultaneous Change

To add to this challenge, it needs to be recognized that complexity/perpetual change increases as the interval of time increases to obtain all the necessary process requirements and/or to execute a given process.

In change science, this is referred to as the change/time continuum principle.

The change/time continuum principle states that change between a beginning existing set of conditions and a subsequent set of conditions occurs in intervals along a change continuum, which is then used as a construct of time.

Therefore, change cannot occur without an interval of change/time.

Consequently, the length of time it takes to execute an implementation or the execution of a process/strategy signifies a major risk. The bottom line is that time represents a major enemy of executives since, the longer the length of the change/time interval, the more risk that is created due to the increase in the amount of change that takes place.

In addition, this change in conditions occurs not only in a given organizational environment but also all around us. The law of simultaneous change states that change is occurring universally and simultaneously everywhere.

This means that as executives, we are not only subject to the risk associated with all the change taking place within our organization but also with all the challenges related to the change occurring outside the organization.

The continuously changing conditions of competitors, government activities, the economy, and more all represent examples of these simultaneous and multi-environmental challenges.

That is why I stress that executives require a methodology that is flexible and can be responsive and effective under multiple conditions and environments.

Effects Of Perpetual Change, Time, And Simultaneous Change

Figure 6.6 is a graphic presentation of how the risk associated with perpetual change resulting in continuously changing conditions increases with the length of time of execution.

Figure 6.7 indicates how this risk in figure 6.6 is amplified when the broader, not just internal dynamics but also external dynamics, are taken into consideration.

Takeaways from figures 6.6 and 6.7:

- Complexity and difficulty increase with time
- Changing conditions equal increasing risk
- The ability to predict future conditions is more and more unrealistic as change/time intervals increase in length
- Time required to execute is your enemy

Figure 6.6

Increasing Risk Over Change/Time

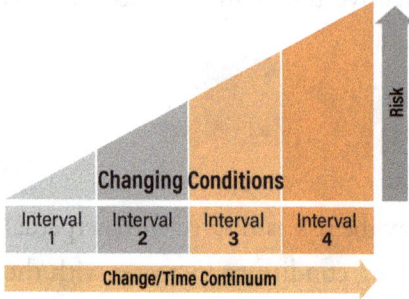

Figure 6.7

Change Occurs Simultaneously Across All Environments

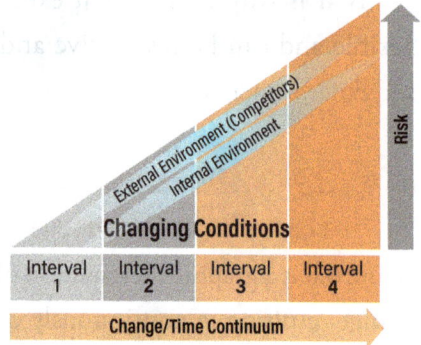

Dynamic Execution Tools

Taken together, the challenges from perpetual change, change/time intervals, and simultaneous change might appear to be interesting conversations but beyond anyone's control.

However, through an understanding of these dynamics and the use of the Dynamic Execution system, these risks can be defined, mitigated, monitored, and controlled, leading to a reduction in risk and increased probability of successfully accomplishing your objectives.

Example: Risk Dynamics Of Traditional Versus A Blended Organization With Feedback Loops

Figure 6.8 indicates how, historically, the traditional perspective viewed strategic execution activities as distinct from daily operations activities. This perspective looks at implementation and strategic execution efforts in the context of projects to be completed.

Figure 6.9 depicts the traditional interaction between daily operations activity and project execution. Execution activities tend to be disrupters to daily operational activities from the start of the project implementation through the completion of the project.

As discussed earlier, these methods develop implementation plans that are then driven down into the organization. The plans tend to follow strict implementation and project management guidelines that are inflexible, act as a major disrupter, can extend the time required to implement, and can create conflicts in organizational priorities, daily operations, and among staff.

However, figure 6.9 also highlights that from a risk perspective, the potential for failure to obtain objectives from these types of approaches increases significantly with the passage of time due to the ever-increasing changes in internal and external conditions.

Figure 6.8

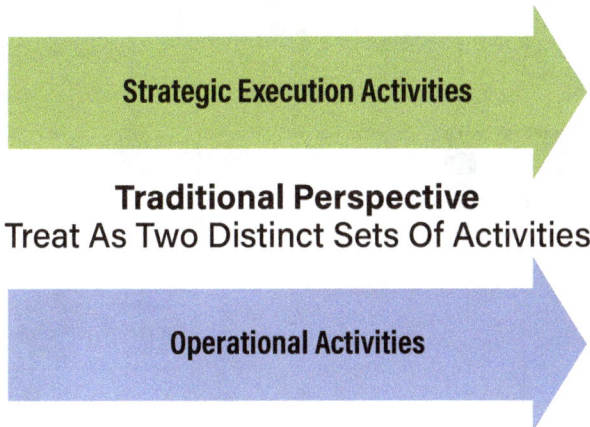

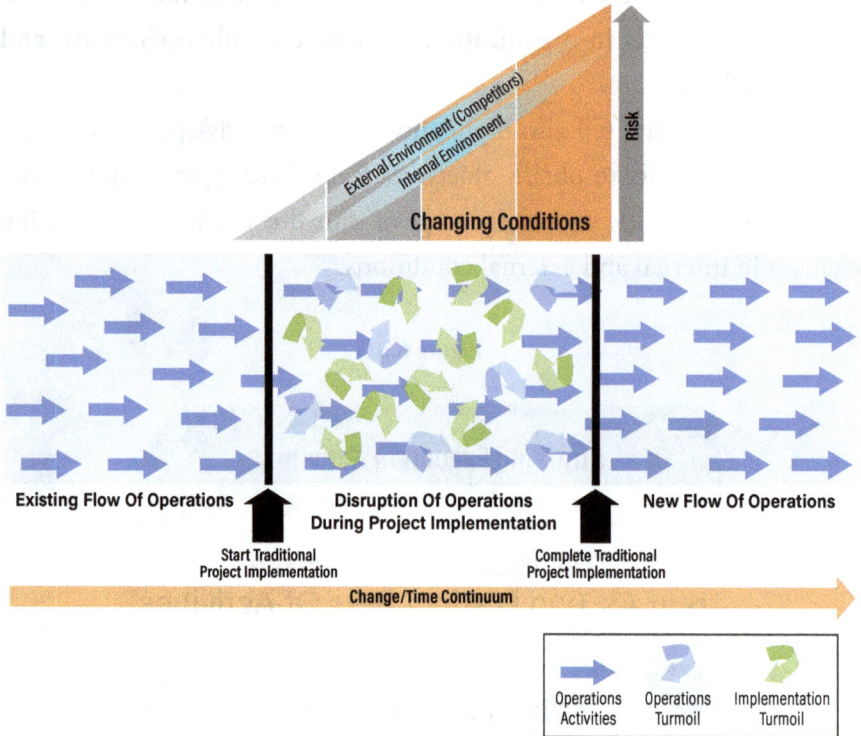

Figure 6.9

Traditional Implementation

Disruptive Interaction Among Strategic And Operations Activities

Figure 6.10 shows the stark contrast to the traditional approach of using the Dynamic Execution blended strategic/operations organization structure. There is a continuous blending of strategic execution activities into daily activities. This not only allows for dynamic scheduling of strategic and operational activities but also supports the ability to have multiple strategic execution initiatives taking place simultaneously.

Figure 6.10

Organization Structure Under Dynamic Execution

Objective Management Not Project Management

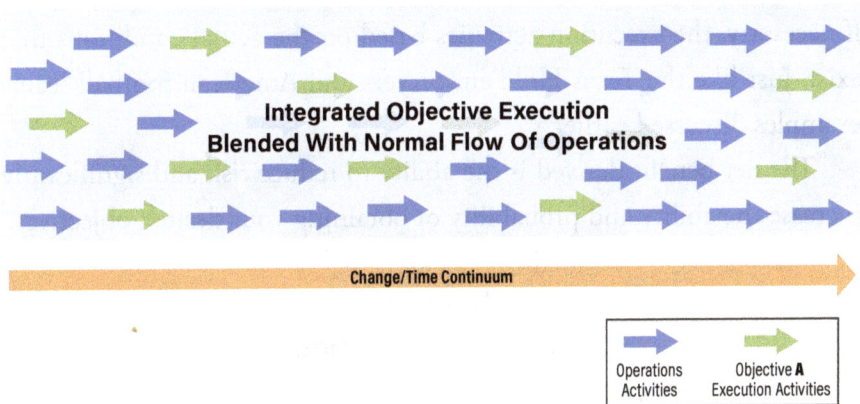

Integrated Objective Execution
Blended With Normal Flow Of Operations

Change/Time Continuum

| Operations Activities | Objective **A** Execution Activities |

Figure 6.11 indicates how feedback loops are included in the daily activities at critical points for disconnect and assumption monitoring, analysis, and control.

The execution of each objective will have its own unique set of feedback loops and data monitoring points. Once again, this supports the ability for simultaneous execution across multiple strategies/objectives.

Figure 6.12 is most noteworthy in that it shows how the use of feedback loops significantly reduces the risk associated with changing conditions over time. This structure can be used to reduce the time interval between critical points in the execution process, thereby reducing the overall change occurring during each interval.

In addition, this methodology provides the organization with the capability to reassess and potentially modify the assumptions, strategy, process, or implementation based on the actual versus assumed or expected conditions that exist.

Just to be clear, as depicted in figure 6.12, the use of continuous monitoring and feedback allows you to incrementally break the change/

time intervals into short periods, thereby reducing the number of changing conditions and associated risks that can affect the execution.

This, in turn, creates a structure whereby the organization and executives can continually, efficiently, and effectively reassess and adjust, if necessary, the execution activities based on the actual conditions that exist, just like the Texas Hold'em players and American football teams examples discussed earlier.

The net benefit derived is the ability to reduce risk and significantly increase the ability and probability of obtaining your desired objectives.

Figure 6.11

Dynamic Execution

Create Monitoring/Analysis Points And Feedback Loops

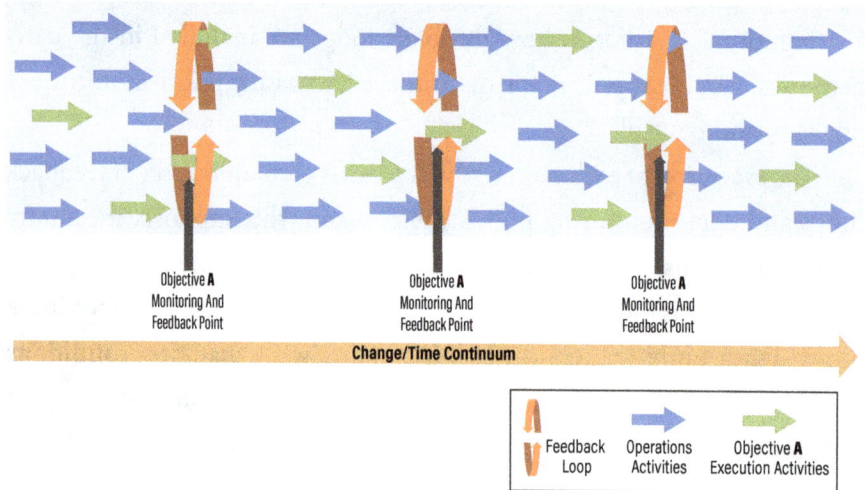

Objective **A** Monitoring And Feedback Point

Objective **A** Monitoring And Feedback Point

Objective **A** Monitoring And Feedback Point

Change/Time Continuum

Feedback Loop — Operations Activities — Objective **A** Execution Activities

Figure 6.12

Dynamic Execution

Risk Of Failure Due To Changing Conditions Is Greatly Reduced

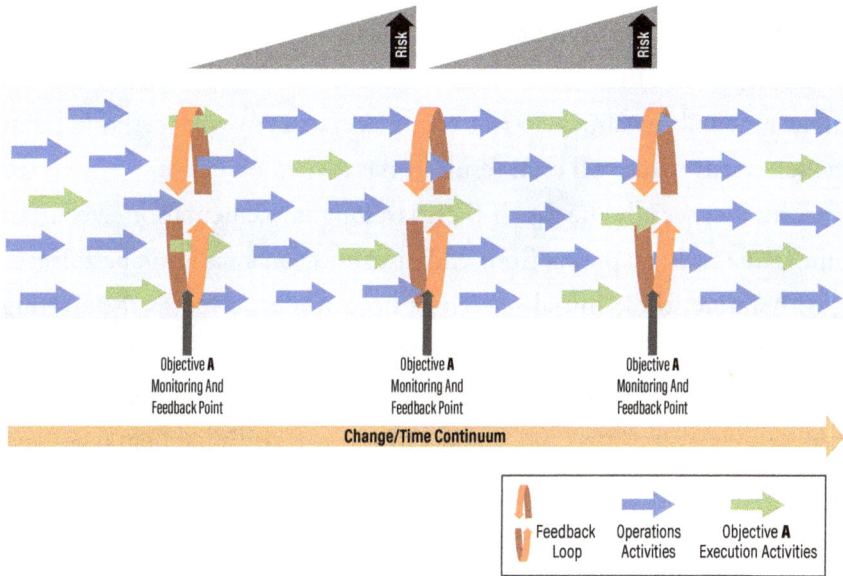

Feedback Loop	Operations Activities	Objective **A** Execution Activities

Summary

The main goal in strategic selection and execution for executives should be to obtain their desired critical objectives.

The risk is when you lock yourself into a rigid implementation or strategic execution methodology, it is easy for the success of that methodology to become the focus versus what is the real critical issue for executives, successfully obtaining the desired objective.

Therefore, the very first risk executives need to recognize and avoid is that the main focus on their desired goal does not get lost because the objective shifts instead to a focus on the successful execution of a specific strategy, implementation plan, or execution methodology.

To some it can sound counterintuitive since in theory, having a successful execution of a specific strategy using a recommended implementation and execution methodology should result in reaching the desired executive objective, especially if there is a great deal of front-end time and effort committed to the selection.

However, given the complexity that exists, there are too many front-end unknowns to give the confidence level required that the selections made are, in fact, the best, unknown conditions do not exist, unexpected environmental dynamics do not take place, or even with certainty, that the selections made will even result in the desired objective.

This is especially the case if there is a long implementation/execution time frame and/or a proper front-end disconnect analysis is not performed.

Therefore, these initial selections need to be viewed as the starting point of a Dynamic Execution process.

As an executive, I received many differing opinions on the pluses and minuses regarding the time it takes to execute an implementation and selected strategy.

Some had justifiable logic, and some often appeared to be self-serving.

The latter were often presented by solution providers, whose fees for services were based upon hours or scope and their ability to staff a project became easier if a project had a long implementation time frame.

However, rather than getting into the specifics of the pluses and minuses, what I have presented above is based upon the science behind change and cuts to the chase: discussing execution time from the perspective of inherent, naturally occurring perpetual change and risk.

It must be recognized that the amount of complexity/perpetual change increases as the interval of time it takes to obtain all the necessary process requirements increases, thereby generating significantly more risk of failure.

In addition, failure to monitor and adjust for inaccurate assumptions and/or unexpected conditions over long periods of time not only represents an additional effort to correct these issues later on in the process but, in the worst case, can lead to a complete inability to execute.

Once again, this is where my concepts, tools, and methods deviate from the traditional and ultimately address the executive risk associated with the time of execution.

A paradigm shift to a blending of strategic initiatives with day-to-day operations provides an opportunity to reduce risk. It allows a shift away from discrete time-dependent project initiatives to a continuous flow of strategic execution that can help avoid many of the time-sensitive issues.

To be clear, the selection of specific strategies and associated implementation requirements will still be necessary. However, the execution will be layered in as part of a continuous blended strategic/operations structure, resulting in flexibility of timing, an ability to simultaneously execute multiple strategic initiatives, and an ability to adjust priorities when necessary and assess and address any associated impacts due to these changes in priorities.

The use of disconnect analysis will not only define the assumptions used and the disconnects that need to be addressed for a selected strategy but will also provide an opportunity to determine time and resource requirements more analytically. This represents an ability to reduce risk by providing critical information in the blending of strategic initiatives with day-to-day operations and establishing critical factors that need to be monitored and controlled during the execution process.

When taken together with a blending of strategic execution with operations and the use of disconnect analysis, the use of feedback loops now creates an organizational closed-loop system of strategic execution. Feedback loops provide the communication flow of strategic initiative information down into the organization and the upward communication of critical considerations and information generated from the ongoing monitoring of critical factors. This communication structure represents an ability to greatly reduce risk, including the risk associated with the length of time to execute. This closed-loop system for strategic initiative development and execution becomes the basis for the Dynamic Execution methodology.

7

What Executives Are Never Taught In School

Functionality Trade-Offs

Illustration: An organization was captivated by the availability of customer self-service bot technology as a way to reduce costs, improve staff efficiency, and streamline the customer experience. However, upon implementation, sales dropped.

Through further analysis, they realized that while one segment of their customer base found the use of this technology acceptable and even desirable, there was also a major demographic of their customer base that preferred human versus technological interaction and moved their business to competitors.

In change science, this is referred to as a functionality trade-off, where there is a selection between two alternative functionalities, which are interconnected in such a way that you cannot obtain the functionality of one alternative without sacrificing the functionality of the other alternative.

Functionality trade-offs can be very common for organizations when the strategic initiative includes the selection and implementation of new enterprise software systems.

It is not unusual for the setup of these systems to require the selection of a specific software configuration that provides a desired functionality to one department but sacrifices or creates major issues in the functionality the software will provide to another department.

Those of you who are familiar with a manufacturing environment might have experienced a situation where a new software system is selected to support an expanded functionality for operations.

For example, the configuration of the bill of material and other technical product information within this new software to support the functionality for operations may, unfortunately, not be consistent with the configuration necessary to support the functionality required by engineering. However, the capability of the software only allows for a single configuration, and therefore, only the desired functionality of one of the departments can prevail.

While it might be hard to imagine, I have seen numerous times where a situation like this operations/engineering functionality trade-off is not fully understood or discovered until after the system has been acquired and major progress on the implementation has already taken place.

This has left the organization in the tough position of either walking away from the software, incurring major unexpected costs and time to modify the software, or, in this case, modifying an enormous amount of engineering data to support the configuration required by operations.

Executives must recognize the risk associated with functionality trade-offs and make sure the organization incorporates the efforts required to determine and properly mitigate these risks. The best place to initiate these efforts is within the disconnect analysis. Incorporation within the disconnect analysis allows the organization to discover potential functionality trade-offs and to determine if any differentiators exist among alternative strategies and implementations under consideration.

Feedback loops are a valuable tool when looking for potential functionality trade-offs. They allow for a targeted downward flow of information regarding the strategic alternatives under consideration and the upward flow of actual conditions and issues (including potential functionality trade-offs). It is important to realize that there is often an untapped existing staff knowledge of potential functionality trade-offs. Unfortunately, this knowledge often gets lost within the selection process methodology used, and a need for a broader, efficient incorporation of necessary feedback.

The key to remember is that both the disconnect analysis and feedback loops rely on understanding the major requirements for each strategic alternative under consideration. It is these requirements, when compared to actual existing conditions, that will, in turn, determine the amount of implementation effort and the potential for functionality trade-offs.

"When Not If" Challenge

Illustration: An organization knew with a high degree of certainty a major customer was going to substantially increase their demand for a product.

To support this increase in demand, the organization determined that it would need to significantly increase the capacity and availability of working capital.

Unfortunately, the product was a new, highly engineered product that would be phasing out an existing product.

These dynamics led to a situation of uncertainty regarding the size and timing of the initial launch of the demand. What I like to refer to from an executive perspective is the "when not if" challenge, where the probability of an event (the "if") occurring is high, but determining the "when" that event will actually occur is difficult.

It is a major challenge because it requires the commitment of a great deal of capital and resources without knowing exactly when the actual sales or other benefits will be available to create the necessary cash flow to support these commitments.

If executed too late, executives run the risk of losing potential revenue and/or creating major customer dissatisfaction.

If executed too early, executives run the risk of exhausting their available resources, such as cash, prematurely creating major financial and credibility issues.

That is what happened in this illustration; I was brought into the organization because the executives miscalculated the "when" and found themselves struggling financially.

Even though special private equity capital and debt arrangements were established in advance to support this growth, the organization found itself in a position of lacking necessary working capital and negative profitability caused by the premature execution of the initiatives required to support this growth.

It should be noted that the issue regarding the failure of the "if" taking place was very minimal. Total first-year sales ultimately grew by over 70 percent after the delayed launch of this product.

Using the Dynamic Execution concepts, we were able to immediately restore profitability, stabilize the relationship with the bank, successfully meet the demands of the customer product launch, and ultimately provide a successful exit strategy for the private equity group.

The "when not if" challenge is very common and can be a major contributor to an organization's inability to survive due to a lack of sufficient capital. A review of the literature indicates that a vast majority of business failures can be traced to a lack of cash or poor cash management.

Additionally, the "when not if" challenge is not just in fast growth scenarios. It is also a common result of the natural maturing of an organization over time, or even more common, the mistiming of the execution of a major strategic initiative.

Even if an organization grows at a reasonable rate, it will reach points in the life cycle where existing systems, capacities, and operational structures start to max out, become antiquated, and need to be replaced.

However, if the strategic initiatives and associated resources are expended prematurely, the organization can run into major financial difficulties, just like the organization highlighted in the above illustration.

On the other hand, if the strategic initiatives are executed too late, the organization can have difficulty in meeting customer requirements, which can also lead to limitations on growth or, even worse, financial difficulties due to a loss of customers.

Example: "When Not If" Under Traditional Approaches

Figures 7.1 through 7.3 indicate the challenges and significant risks executives face under traditional execution approaches and methodologies to "when not if" challenges.

These risks are created from the differences in (a) the timing between the completion date of a project that results in the accomplishment of an objective and (b) the date the benefits from the opportunities associated with that objective are available.

I would argue that in many, if not most, cases, executives are not even aware of the true level of the risks, challenges, or exposure to these dynamics.

Figure 7.1 represents the ideal that is either consciously or unconsciously built into the creation and execution launch of a new objective.

The completion of the execution of the launch of an objective occurs exactly when the benefits to be derived from the objective are available to the organization.

Figure 7.1:
Timing Of Available Benefits = Completion Date Of Project

Under this scenario, the organization has not consumed unnecessary time or resources by prematurely executing the objective. Nor has the organization failed to recognize any of the benefits to be derived by completing the execution after the benefits are initially available.

Figure 7.1 indicates how the organization has established, based on its implementation plan, the required resources necessary to fully execute what is generally referred to as the project.

As the project progresses on the timeline through the implementation, those resources are utilized until the implementation/project is complete.

As then indicated, in the ideal, the completion takes place perfectly timed to when actual benefits from the opportunities associated with the objective are available to the organization.

These benefits, through such things as increased revenues or cost reductions, ultimately generate positive cash generation and a rebuilding of available resources within the organization.

Figure 7.1

Traditional Implementation

"When Not If" — Ideal Timing

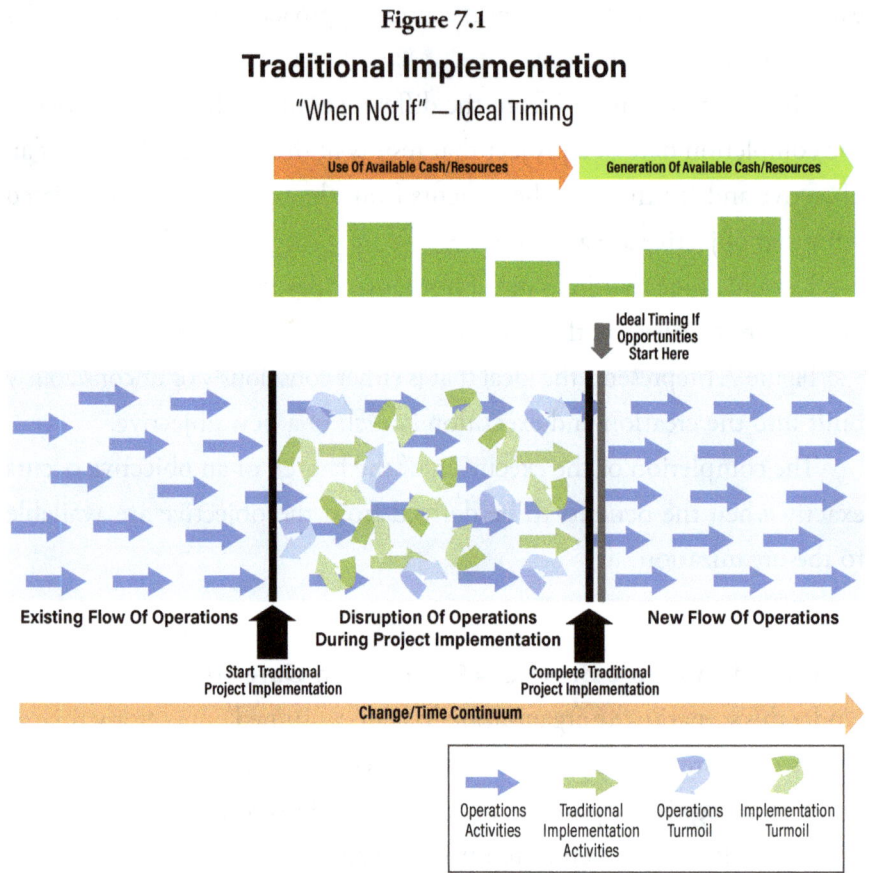

Figures 7.2 and 7.3 demonstrate what happens if the date of availability of the benefits derived from the opportunities exists either earlier or after the project completion date. There are three very commonly occurring scenarios where this occurs.

One, the planned completion date and availability of benefits from the opportunities originally matched up (i.e., are the ideals in figure 7.1). However, for whatever reason, the actual execution completion date moves forward or backward in timing.

Two, the planned completion date and availability of benefits from the opportunities originally matched up (i.e., are the ideals in figure 7.1). However, for whatever reason, the actual availability of opportunity benefits date moves forward or backward in timing.

Third, there are inaccuracies or lack of consideration regarding the date of the availability of the opportunity benefits when the planned completion date is originally determined for the project. Therefore, the completion of the project is inappropriately scheduled without consideration before or after the start of the benefits derived from the opportunity.

These scenarios are common because project completion dates and implementation plans tend to be strictly scheduled and planned out.

Figure 7.2 presents what happens if the date the benefits are available from an opportunity occurs before the completion date of the project.

Figure 7.2: Timing Of Available Benefits Are Earlier Than Completion Date Of Project

Once again, figure 7.2 indicates how the organization has established, based upon their implementation plan, the required resources necessary to fully execute the project and derive the organizational objective.

As in figure 7.1, as the project progresses along the timeline through the implementation, there is a utilization of those resources until the implementation/project is complete, at which time there is the potential for positive cash generation.

However, given that the availability date of the benefits that can be derived from an executed objective is before the completion date, figure 7.2 demonstrates how there is a loss of positive cash generation opportunity.

In addition, besides the loss of unrecognized benefits, an organization's inability to meet expectations can also create the potential for negative reactions from customers, the marketplace, or financial institutions.

Figure 7.2

Traditional Implementation

"When Not If" — Opportunity Starts Before Completion

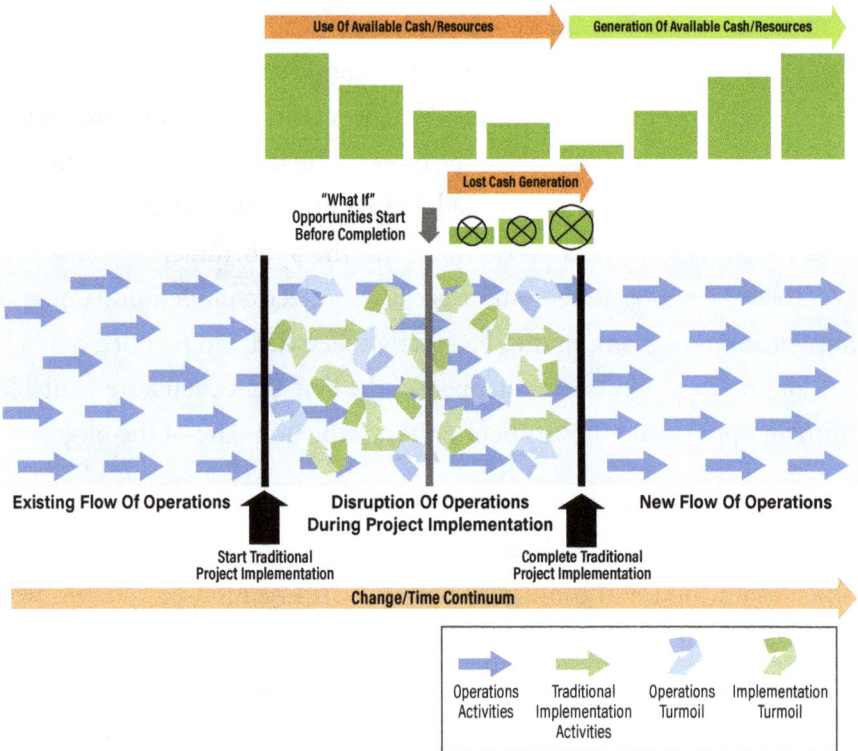

Figure 7.3 presents another major risk to the organization. It is when the date the benefits from an opportunity are available occurs after the completion date of the project.

Figure 7.3: Timing Of Available Benefits Are Later Than Completion Date Of Project

This scenario is consistent with the illustration I discussed earlier and can lead to major financial issues.

As seen in figure 7.3, an organization holds to the timing embedded in its implementation plan to obtain the completion of the objective.

Unfortunately, this completion date was premature of the date associated with an ability to derive benefits from the expected opportunity.

Therefore, the organization exhausts its available resources and faces additional risk associated with the negative utilization of additional resources until such a date as the benefits from the opportunity are available.

This can create a major financial ripple effect within the organization and a potential loss of credibility with financial institutions.

Figure 7.3

Traditional Implementation

"When Not If" — Opportunity Starts After Completion

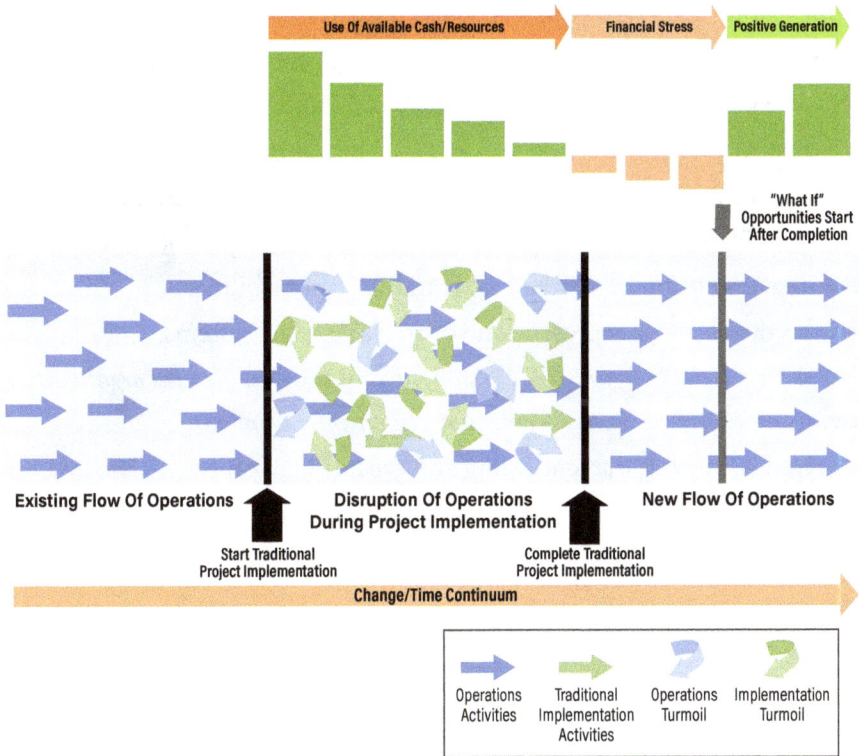

Use Of Available Cash/Resources   Financial Stress   Positive Generation

"What If"
Opportunities Start
After Completion

Existing Flow Of Operations   Disruption Of Operations During Project Implementation   New Flow Of Operations

Start Traditional Project Implementation   Complete Traditional Project Implementation

Change/Time Continuum

| Operations Activities | Traditional Implementation Activities | Operations Turmoil | Implementation Turmoil |

Example: "When Not If" Under Change Science Dynamic Execution

There are innovative concepts and tools available to assist executives in effectively tackling "when not if" challenges.

Again, my approach to "when not if" challenges begins by leveraging a blended strategic execution and operations organization structure combined with the utilization of feedback loops. These become the foundation for dynamic scheduling, which I will introduce here but explore in more detail elsewhere.

Figure 7.4 revisits what a blended strategic/operations structure looks like.

As discussed, all individuals within the organization are trained and assigned various commitment levels of time and strategic execution responsibilities in conjunction with their daily operational execution responsibilities. However, these commitments are intended to be flexible, with a level of empowerment attached to them.

Just like in the existing world of scheduling operational activities, an organization must establish the tools and systems to support the communication, scheduling, and execution necessary to be successful in the dual execution of strategic/operations responsibilities.

Feedback loops represent one of those support systems.

As indicated in figure 7.4, Dynamic Execution in a blended organization focuses on objective management, not project management.

In this context, the scheduling and execution of objectives becomes no different than the scheduling of customer demand for services or products.

Figure 7.4

Organization Structure Under Dynamic Execution

Objective Management Not Project Management

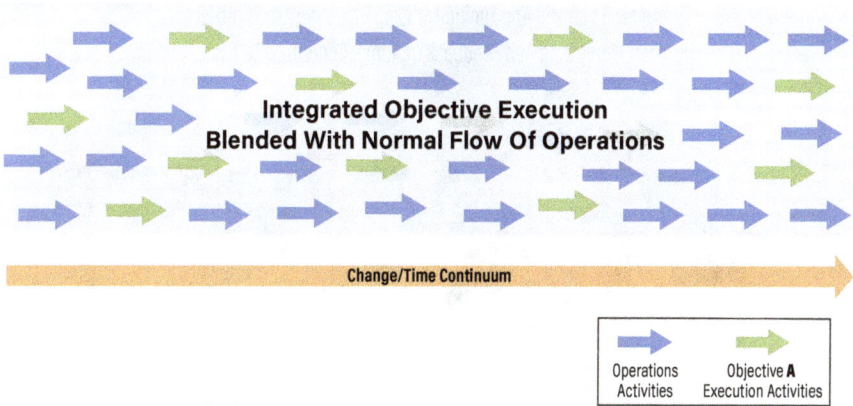

Figure 7.5 demonstrates how the power of a blended organization structure explodes with the recognition that a superior environment is created for the simultaneous execution of multiple objectives.

With the incorporation of feedback loops, the execution and timing for multiple objectives can be throttled based on the monitoring and analysis of actual conditions against critical factors and assumptions.

As depicted in figure 7.5, each objective has its own set of monitoring and analysis points along with associated feedback loops. This creates a capability to dynamically look at the status of objectives at any point in time individually, in relationship to all other objectives, and/or in the interrelationship between objectives and operational demands.

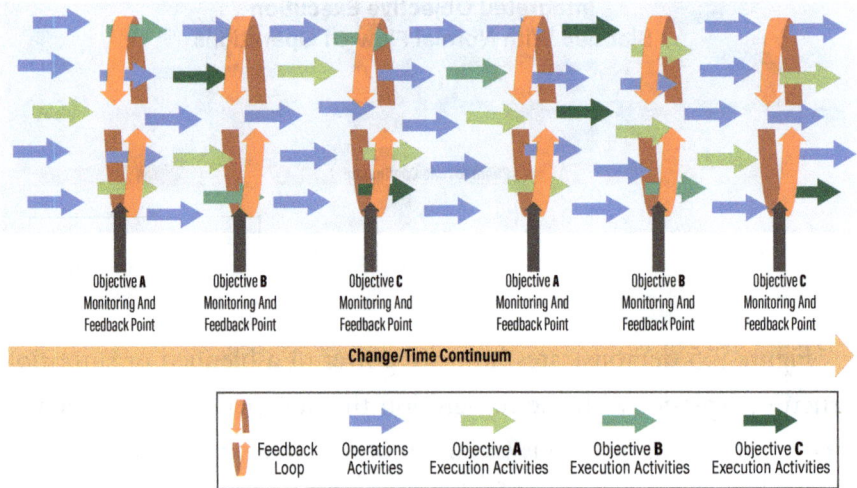

Figure 7.5

Dynamic Execution

Provides Ability To Simultaneously Execute Multiple Objectives

Execution Efforts And Timing For Each Objective Are Throttled
Based Upon Monitoring And Feedback Of Actual Conditions To Assumptions

Finally, figure 7.6 depicts how this blended structure, feedback loops, and dynamic scheduling provide the ability to throttle the execution of objectives, creating an innovative solution set to address "when not if" challenges.

Based on the feedback received, the progress of any given objective is performed in a context that conserves resources while continually positioning it for the possibility of accelerated or delayed execution.

Even if resource requirements are identical to those of a traditional implementation plan, this solution set provides an improved ability to determine and react to shifting opportunity timelines while conserving cash and minimizing execution time, thereby maximizing opportunity benefits.

While not fail-proof, this dynamic methodology significantly reduces executive risk exposure to "when, not if" challenges.

Figure 7.6

Dynamic Execution

"When Not If" – Ability To Match Completion With Opportunity Date

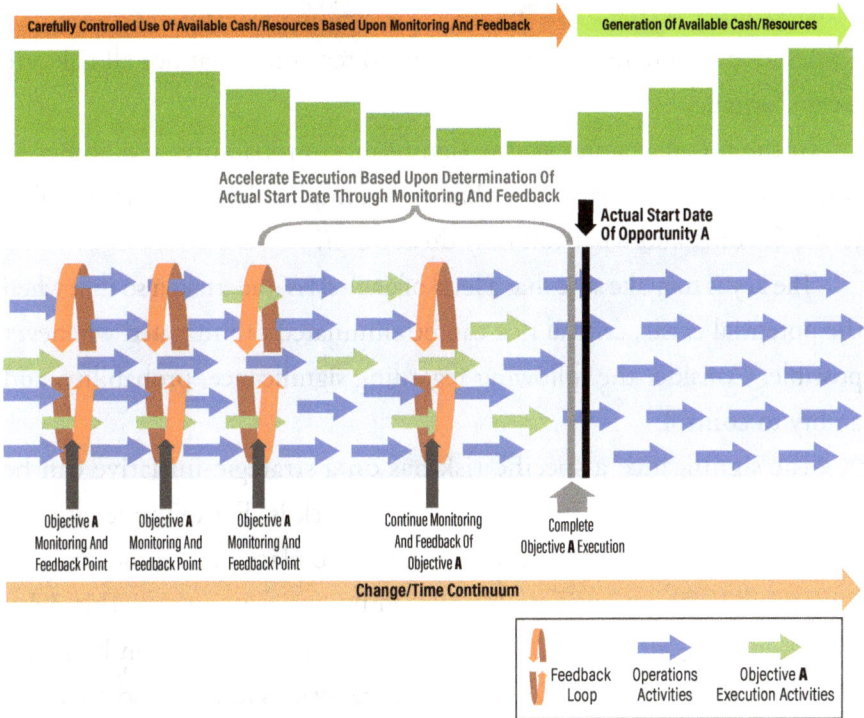

To reiterate, figure 7.6 shows how the progress of the execution for Objective A is embedded within the daily strategic/operations activities. However, Objective A execution activities are throttled based upon the most current information/conditions that exist at each monitoring/feedback loop point, which includes the most up-to-date status information/conditions associated with the expected "when date" for the available benefits derived from the launch of Objective A.

Therefore, as the "when date" solidifies, the activities associated with the execution of Objective A can be adjusted so as to match the actual date of the start of the available benefits. This allows executives and their organization to conserve and efficiently utilize resources while maximizing the benefits derived from the launch of Objective A and minimizing the potential negative issues related to a premature or late launch.

Eliminate And Mitigate

To describe the obvious, it is important to recognize that not all risks are created equal.

In the broadest context, the significance, probability, and ability to control a given risk varies. But what are the implications of this variability to the C-suite, and what can they do about it?

The key is to make sure that a level of analysis is undertaken so that when the potential exists, critical risk can be eliminated or mitigated whenever possible. Consider the following regarding significance, probability, and ability to control.

The significance a specific risk has on a strategic initiative can be different depending on what the particular risk is. For example, assume an execution of some event that needs to take place during the strategic initiative has the potential to be delayed by one day (a risk). This delay would, in turn, affect the timing of completing the execution by a day. However, this risk of a one-day delay is probably insignificant and can easily be compensated for. On the other hand, if the delay in the event turns into weeks, then the level of significance/impact of this risk might increase substantially. The advantage of assessing the impact of the various specific risk exposures is that it helps filter out the risk that has low significance while focusing on the risk that signifies the greatest potential impact on the objective to be obtained.

Just like significance, the level of probability that a specific risk will occur can influence the level of effort and concentration we want to place on that particular risk. However, having a risk that has a high probability in and by itself may not be an issue. This is due to the fact that unless the probability of a risk is also associated with the significance of that specific risk, it will be difficult to determine the true ramifications associated with the probability.

A big mistake is looking at risk in a homogeneous context, not paying attention to what is controllable versus uncontrollable. One of the easiest ways to manage, control, and reduce risk is to separate and analyze it into two categories: controllable and uncontrollable. It is a sad situation when there is a negative impact on a strategic initiative caused by a risk that has the potential to either be eliminated or mitigated. Unfortunately, I have seen this situation transpire more times than I want to count.

The analysis of risk from the perspective of being controllable and uncontrollable can be built into the disconnect analysis and becomes the starting point for the avoidance of these negative situations.

The first question that should be explored when dealing with controllable risk is: Are there ways to eliminate the controllable risk? Since controllable risk is a risk that is subject to an organization's direct influence, controllable risk should be eliminated whenever possible. This should apply not only to highly significant and probable risk but also to any controllable risk that can be justified from a time, effort, and cost perspective. The elimination of controllable risk is often low-hanging fruit and represents an easy way to reduce risk.

Unlike controllable risk, where the potential for some sort of direct influence exists, no such capability exists in the case of uncontrollable risk. Therefore, uncontrollable risk represents any risk for which direct influence is outside of the control of the organization. The sad situation with uncontrollable risk is that organizations often assume that because the risk is uncontrollable, there is nothing they can do, and they must live with the ramifications.

However, if we want to manage, influence, and reduce risk, then this perspective is not acceptable, especially in cases where the risk is of high significance and moderate to high probability. Instead, the proper perspective should be one of mitigation. While certain risks might be outside of an organization's direct control (for example, the weather and the actions of other organizations), that does not mean that there is not an opportunity to mitigate the risk if it should occur.

I like to refer to this as a form of strategic initiative protectionism. This is developing a plan that, if executed, has the potential to counter the impacts of an uncontrollable risk if and when it occurs.

In addition to the initial activities performed as part of the disconnect analysis, feedback loops provide a substantial capability for the elimination and mitigation of risk. Feedback loops represent a highly effective built-in continuous strategic execution tool to recognize, monitor, and control the elimination and mitigation of controllable and uncontrollable risks.

In summary, eliminate and mitigate is the concept that risk can be viewed in the context of risk factors that are both controllable and uncontrollable.

Suppose you have a controllable risk factor. In that case, that risk factor should be eliminated, provided the significance of the risk factor justifies the time, effort, and cost of elimination.

However, if the risk factor is uncontrollable, then, when possible, that risk factor should be mitigated, provided the significance of the risk factor justifies the time, effort, and cost of mitigation.

The following figure 7.7 depicts the interrelationships between probability and significance, along with some suggested potential high-level actions. A significance of high means an inability to obtain the C-suite objective. A significance of medium means the potential for a major disruption, including the possibility that the objective will not be obtained. A significance of low means minor disruption to the ability to obtain an objective, which is anticipated to be easily correctable if the risk occurs.

Figure 7.7

Risk Assessment And Response Matrix

Risk Assessment	Probability Of A Specific Risk = High	Probability Of A Specific Risk = Medium	Probability Of A Specific Risk = Low
Significance Of Risk = High	Requires a high level of attention and a detailed eliminate/mitigate action plan.	Requires a high level of attention and a detailed eliminate/mitigate action plan.	Eliminate/mitigate risk where cost is justified and monitor closely during execution.
Significance Of Risk = Medium	Requires a high level of attention and a detailed eliminate/mitigate action plan.	Requires a high level of attention and a detailed eliminate/mitigate action plan.	Eliminate/mitigate risk where cost is justified and monitor closely during execution.
Significance Of Risk = Low	Eliminate/mitigate risk where effort is minimal.	Eliminate/mitigate risk where effort is minimal.	Little to no attention or effort.

Summary

The following summary will help reinforce our discussion of *risk* from an executive's perspective.

The starting point in reducing risk is for executives to focus the organization on the use of a disconnect analysis that includes a determination and analysis of assumptions across various strategic alternatives. As discussed, the determination, documentation, monitoring, and, ultimately, control of critical disconnects and assumptions provide a major tool for executives to reduce risk and increase their potential for successful results.

Comprehensive top-to-bottom integrated feedback loops have become an excellent way to increase the ability to accurately determine requirements, actual conditions, and disconnects. They also provide the communications capability necessary for ongoing and timely monitoring and analysis of critical factors. This allows executives and the organization to quickly address and react to any issues that arise from inaccurate, changing, or missing critical assumptions or conditions.

The closed-loop system created by an organization that uses (a) blended strategic execution with operations, (b) disconnect analysis, and (c) feedback loops is one of the best ways executives can address the risk issues associated with the time it takes to develop and execute a strategic initiative. This closed-loop system becomes the basis for Dynamic Execution, and time becomes a critical factor for analysis, monitoring, and control. *In turn, this closed-loop structure represents an ability to greatly reduce the risk associated with the length of time to execute.*

The incorporation of feedback loops into the organization by executives and the human resource management methodology outlined in chapters 8 through 11 will provide a major capability to mitigate the risks associated with staff participation and commitment to strategic initiatives. The key is the seamless blending of strategic initiative activities into the day-to-day operational responsibilities all the way down to the individual level.

The human resource management methodology allows the organization to incorporate the communication of strategic initiative activities and opportunities and, just as importantly, reinforce expectations and evaluate actual participation all the way down to the individual level. Feedback loops then address the ongoing participation of individuals in strategic development and execution activities through the proper level of integration of associated communications into each individual's day-to-day activities.

Finally, not all risks are created equal. Some risks are more controllable than other risks, and the significance and probability of risk can differ considerably. Therefore, an organizational focus by executives on an ongoing analysis and the ability to eliminate or mitigate certain risks can greatly increase the potential to obtain their desired objectives. The significance and probability of risk should be evaluated, and when appropriate, a given risk should be eliminated or mitigated whenever feasible. This should be an analysis that starts as a part of the disconnect analysis and strategic selection and continues all the way through the execution process, fed by the information received via ongoing monitoring and feedback.

PART III

Dynamic Execution Foundational Pillar

Staff Structure / Communications / Evaluations

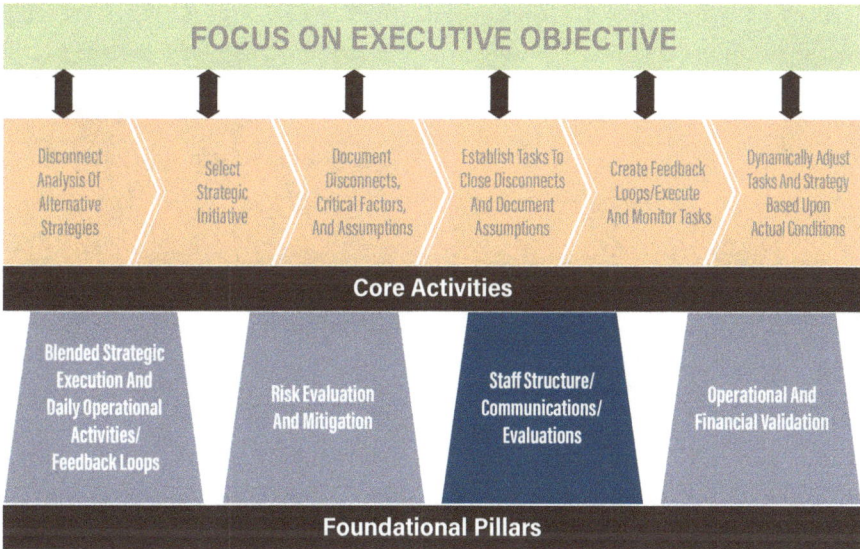

FOCUS ON EXECUTIVE OBJECTIVE

| Disconnect Analysis Of Alternative Strategies | Select Strategic Initiative | Document Disconnects, Critical Factors, And Assumptions | Establish Tasks To Close Disconnects And Document Assumptions | Create Feedback Loops/Execute And Monitor Tasks | Dynamically Adjust Tasks And Strategy Based Upon Actual Conditions |

Core Activities

| Blended Strategic Execution And Daily Operational Activities/ Feedback Loops | Risk Evaluation And Mitigation | Staff Structure/ Communications/ Evaluations | Operational And Financial Validation |

Foundational Pillars

Chapters 8, 9, 10, and 11 provide an executive guide to innovative concepts and approaches to staff structure, communications, and evaluations.

8

Staff Communications And Solitaire

Illustration: My mother loved to play solitaire.

One day, I was preparing for a meeting with the entire organizational team regarding some major strategic initiatives that were going to be launched. I knew that for many, these initiatives represented a significant change.

From experience, I knew I would struggle with how to best address such a large crowd, as all of them had the underlying potential for second-guessing, pushback, and anxiety.

That is when I remembered my mom's love for solitaire and how solitaire might help me with my dilemma. After all, solitaire is easy to understand, and almost everyone I know has played it.

So, I started my meeting by pulling a deck of cards out of my pocket.

After proceeding to remove the deck of cards from the box, I asked the team: "How many times do you think you will have to play solitaire before you win?"

As you might expect, the responses I received were all over the board, and the rationale I received from some of the team members was very logical.

At that point, I proceeded to pull two aces out of my pocket and told them that the correct answer was: "You will never be able to win at solitaire with this deck of cards. You are missing two of the aces."

Then, I explained the following.

"Rarely does anyone in an organization have all the cards in the deck. So, if you second-guess the decisions or push back on the direction being taken, please do so knowing your conclusions are almost certainly based upon missing some of the cards in the deck. While, as a chief executive, I am probably in the best position to have all the cards in the deck, it would be a mistake on my part not to be open to your feedback that might, in fact, provide me with cards I might be missing." (As a side note, my mother always assumed she might be missing cards and counted the cards in the deck before she played her first game.)

"Therefore, I will try to provide as many cards to you as possible as long as it does not jeopardize confidential or strategic market information. In return, I ask that you remain open-minded and committed to the successful execution of our direction and, by all means, provide me with feedback on any cards you feel I might be missing from my deck.

"However, while I truly want everyone's feedback and input, please do not lose commitment if that feedback does not appear to you to have any impact on the decisions or process. There are almost certainly some cards you will still be missing, but that does not mean your continued commitment and feedback is not important."

Inherent Executive Concerns Regarding Staff Communications

I know you are interested in exactly how to create a blended strategic execution and operations organization structure along with associated feedback loops.

However, I also know that, right about now, many executives are struggling with how and what information to share and feedback to solicit from your staff.

So, I will address that discussion first.

As executives, we all have inherent concerns about sharing information with our team.

"Is there a real benefit to sharing information and soliciting feedback, and if so, what is it? If I share information, will my audience fully understand it enough to provide the feedback and commitment I seek?

"How do we avoid giving away confidential or strategic information and yet still obtain the feedback and commitment from the team that is needed for a successful execution?

"How can I address the impacts associated with second-guessing and pushback from my team?

"How can I address the impacts on my communications of the ever-changing environment taking place within the organization? For example, how do I efficiently and effectively keep everyone in the loop, and what are the possible impacts of the use of outdated information?

"How can I address the impacts associated with the anxiety associated with the changes that will take place?"

To address these types of issues, I would like to review some of my observations and experiences.

Benefits, Feedback, And Commitment

Whether we like it or not, observations, interpretations, and discussions among the staff in the organization are constantly taking place.

Unfortunately, as in my solitaire example, much of this intraorganizational chatter, almost for certain, is not cognizant of the missing cards from the solitaire deck.

However, having communication just to meet some sort of perceived communication requirement or as an attempt to discredit the normal organizational chatter that is taking place is not a very productive objective.

Successful communication supports the execution of strategy that results in improved organizational performance. It is not convincing everyone that what you are doing is right.

Therefore, the objective for the executive should be to focus the communications and the disbursement of information and data toward the critical issues and initiatives you are trying to address. You do not need to try to control the narrative and direction of all the conversations occurring in the organization; you only need to control those most relevant conversations for the support you require.

Besides, contrary to what many believe, there is rarely any value in providing unnecessary or irrelevant information, which can often become counterproductive. Many studies indicate that money is not always the number one driver of an individual's satisfaction or engagement. Having a feeling of accomplishment, recognition for achieving something, and working with others toward a successful outcome are often viewed as more significant than pay.

Therefore, communications centered on these desires of achievement, recognition, and working toward a common objective are the best ways to obtain the engagement you are looking for.

Finally, there should always be an attempt to make communications as understandable as possible. Unfortunately, that will not always equate to a clear understanding by all the staff at the individual level. However, this fact helps us recognize the power of the continuous blending of strategic initiatives with day-to-day operations and the use of feedback loops.

Feedback loops and a blended strategic/operations structure provide a continuous communications vehicle—a vehicle that not only helps recognize and address a lack of understanding but also uncovers potential unknown issues and opportunities.

Confidentiality

An interesting case study discussing confidentiality was presented in the series *The Food that Built America* on the HISTORY Channel. It described how, while Post was the original developer of the pop-up toaster pastry, due to the length of time Post had to execute their product launch, Kellogg's Pop-Tart became the actual market leader.[7]

I have already mentioned how execution time is a critical factor in obtaining successful strategic executions.

Therefore, for our purposes here, we need to recognize that ensuring the shortest execution time possible is your best weapon against the risks of not maintaining confidentiality or obtaining a strategic market execution advantage.

We also need to remember that nobody can be 100 percent trusted, and there is always risk from unintentional actions. There is always the risk of staff turnover, and as in the Post/Kellogg's example, there are unintentional missteps.

Even confidentiality agreements in today's environment often represent limited protection.

Speed of execution will always be the executive's number one defense against these risks.

Another observation is that almost everyone understands that certain things are confidential (as the saying goes, "above my pay grade"). Therefore, a simple "I really cannot discuss that" is almost always sufficient. However, that does not mean that staff communications need to be nonexistent.

Instead, if there is a high degree of confidentiality surrounding a given strategic initiative, time must be committed to analyzing the initiative for both what is and is not confidential and at what point the execution process the greatest risk of exposure exists. Beneficial communications can then be tailored to reduce, eliminate, or mitigate the confidentiality risks.

Finally, a pragmatic approach to confidentiality needs to be adopted. To some, almost everything is confidential. It is not uncommon for information to be treated as confidential because it gives the holder a feeling of power when, in reality, the sharing of this information would be beneficial to the accomplishment of an organization's performance.

I tend to find that people want to know their status and accomplishments, and not necessarily all the specifics. They want to know what worked and what did not work and how their efforts made a difference or can make a difference.

Unless there is some sort of incentive system associated with financial information, staff are often more likely to be less interested in whether the organization made $50,000 or $500,000 and more interested in how their organization is performing compared to its competitors. Or, they want to know how successful their involvement was in that last initiative to increase sales or increase delivery of products.

Bottom line, much of the stress related to the communication of confidential information can be reduced by executing confidential initiatives as fast as possible, being realistic about what is and what is not confidential, and focusing on communications required for staff motivation and involvement in successful execution of strategy that results in improved organizational performance.

Second-Guessing And Pushback

Besides the inherent nature of organizational chatter, I have found that there are three main drivers of second-guessing and pushback. The first is a lack of information. This creates an actual or perceived potential for an impending negative impact on those who are second-guessing or pushing back.

The best way to address this situation is to provide the accurate information required and to have open communication about the concerns being presented. (See the discussion on anxiety below.)

A second driver is a subtle type of second-guessing and pushback that I like to refer to as passive resistance. There is no outward or aggressive posture toward the efforts in this situation. Instead, there is a lack of engagement and minimal to no effort to support the required activities. Interestingly, this often occurs with individuals who are considered good and quality performers. They take this approach because they are very busy and have seen a history of so many projects that are initially claimed to be important but ultimately just go away with no success and little to no ramifications.

Therefore, because of their workload, they take a "wait-and-see" (passive resistance) approach. This approach does not outwardly appear to be a lack of support when, in reality, they are sitting back to see if it is just another flash-in-the-pan project. Once again, this situation can be resolved with a *strong ongoing commitment* to the continuous blending of strategic initiatives with day-to-day operations methodology. In this case, success breeds engagement.

Finally, in the third driver, there are sometimes individuals who will not positively engage, no matter what or how you attempt to solicit their support or involvement. These can be both well-performing and poorly-performing individuals and can be the result of any number of reasons, including (a) a desire just to do their job and that is all, (b) work/life balance, (c) just having a bad attitude or having a job they have no real interest in. Often, the best way to handle these situations, especially for those good performers, is to communicate that a lack of involvement in their case is acceptable, but pushback or failing to cooperate when needed or to follow required procedures will not be acceptable.

As with the discussion on anxiety below, it is also a good idea to still have open dialogue, provide information, and at least review their position to make sure there are no missing conditions that should be taken into consideration.

No matter how great you believe the content and structure of your communications are, you will rarely, if ever, get 100 percent buy-in or belief in your intended message. However, 100 percent buy-in is not as important as your ability to positively reach those resources who are most critical for the success of your objectives. Rarely is participation by everyone in the organization important for accomplishing an objective.

Therefore, try to focus the communications relative to specific initiatives toward those resources who are most critical for success. This does not mean there is no value in informing the broader organization in general terms what is happening. After all, there might be someone you are not aware of with a card you are missing from your deck. However, a lack of communication with those who you know might be critical for success would be very unfortunate and, therefore, should be the focus of your communications effort.

Ever-Changing Environment

By now, you can already surmise what I will say about staff communications in a world of changing environmental dynamics—embrace the power of the continuous blending of strategic initiatives with day-to-day operations and feedback loop methodology.

This philosophy and methodology are structured to intrinsically be dynamic and responsive to changing conditions.

That is why they are considered a major component of the overall Dynamic Execution system.

Anxiety

Anxiety is often a hidden risk factor for a successful execution.

I have observed how a lack of understanding, discussion, and consideration of anxiety by executives can be a major contributor to difficulties in executing strategic change.

It can also lead to missed opportunities relative to staff involvement and productive input.

Unfortunately, this is probably driven by the perception that anxiety is a naturally occurring complex issue that needs to be left to the professionals.

Fortunately, there are simplified concepts that, when understood, can improve the executive's ability to address some of this anxiety while at the same time even finding positive opportunities.

To start, we need to look at some drivers of anxiety.

The greater the significance level a change represents, the greater the level of potential anxiety that will exist. For example, changing a process that could affect the on-time launch of a new service offering will create far more anxiety than a simple change in a process associated with the daily removal of trash from office receptacles.

We need to recognize that no matter how you want to personally define difficulty, the more difficulty you have associated with a change the more likely you are to experience anxiety. For example, a change requiring communication in multiple languages is more difficult than a change where you can communicate in a common language.

We are more likely to experience less anxiety when we are in control as opposed to when we are not in control. For example, using staff who are directly under your control to accomplish a critical change that you are responsible for will generally produce less anxiety than having to rely on staffing under someone else's control.

In addition, a lack of control can also be associated with the unknown. Even though a change might be simple, if a change contains a lot of unknowns, the unknowns create a feeling of a lack of control. This then increases the potential for anxiety. For example, offering a product or service for the first time represents contending with many unknowns compared to providing a known product or service. All these possible unknowns associated with these new efforts greatly increase the potential for anxiety.

It is also important to realize that significance, difficulty, and control are not just individual characteristics but are, in fact, dynamics that can interact with each other relative to the same change. For example, a change can be very significant, but if you believe that you have a great deal of control over the event, then the anxiety that might otherwise exist can be tempered or even completely negated.

Finally, we must recognize that at the heart of anxiety is the realization that based upon prior experiences, no matter how a change is executed, there is no guarantee that execution will be successful. In addition, if it is successful, there might be some negative ramifications.

If change were guaranteed to always take place with no negative ramifications, then there would be no reason to have any anxiety. However, through experience, everyone recognizes that change with no negative ramifications to them is difficult to guarantee.

Through these experiences, individuals develop perceptions as to the ramifications and potential effects associated with significance, difficulty, and control. Therefore, an inherent defense mechanism in the form of anxiety is created.

From an executive perspective, when considering the structure and content of staff communication, there is a benefit to the understanding of the potential for, and basis behind, anxiety within the organization.

Through this understanding, communication structures can be tailored to preemptively address expected anxiety hot spots. They can also be used to help in an analysis of the drivers and conditions creating anxiety that might represent critical factors (i.e., unknown missing cards from the deck) that will need to be addressed during the execution process.

In the end, having a handle on the understanding of anxiety will improve the potential to avoid issues and obtain a successful execution.

9

Staff Communications Concepts And Tools

We need to start with a basic important premise and will use the following example that I think many executives will be able to relate to.

Illustration: Over my career, I cannot even count the number of staff incentive, performance, and compensation structures I have been exposed to.

From the most basic to the most sophisticated, from the trendy to the most established, and from the most skeptical to the most progressive, I have found a common denominator that summarizes the often-unrecognized capability of an organization's staff. Through experience, I have concluded that you can give a room full of business experts a year to create the best compensation structure possible, and I will give my staff at any level in the organization three days to figure out how to beat the system.

So, when discussing staff communications or anything else involving staff's capability for understanding, the important basic premise to start with is that an organization's staff are intuitively intelligent. They should not be underestimated in their ability to understand and dissect information to exceed expectations.

With this in mind, and using the observations and experiences discussed in the prior chapter as background, we can explore some actual executive concepts and tools to use relative to staff communications that support the continuous blending of strategic initiatives with day-to-day operations and feedback loop methodology.

Establishment Of Feedback Loops

Feedback loops need to be bidirectional, feeding information down into the organization regarding strategic change drivers, assumptions, and goals while soliciting information up through the organization regarding actual existing conditions, the status of activities, and the monitoring of assumptions.

Feedback loops need to be continuous to obtain a constant ongoing process of blending strategic initiatives with day-to-day activities.

Continuous commitment also communicates seriousness about the ongoing importance and commitment of everyone's efforts and involvement.

Therefore, feedback loops represent a communication structure that is more than just special meetings or occasional updates; instead, communication is integrated into normal daily activities. Individuals must realize that the success of the organization requires ongoing top-to-bottom improvements to operations, which, in turn, are dependent on the ongoing successful execution of strategic initiatives. Consequently, their responsibilities will need to include strategic execution, monitoring, and feedback responsibilities in addition to day-to-day operational responsibilities.

Obviously, the balance between the level of these two responsibilities must be defined by the organization. It can change based on the specific activities taking place at any point in time.

This balance can and will vary by the position and individual within the organization.

Generally, there is a shift toward greater strategic responsibility the higher up one goes on the organization chart.

In the ideal, the objective is for feedback loops to become seamless so that all staff come to feel that, at some level, participation in strategic execution is a normal part of their job while still supporting a balance with their other daily operational activities.

To accomplish this, feedback loops should be non-threatening so that participation is positive and fosters a desire to contribute and be engaged in improving organizational performance. Feedback loops should be factual and open to communicating both positive and negative information, along with accomplishments, missteps, and reasons behind changes in direction. (Like it or not, staff will quickly see through filtered or inaccurate information.)

Other Considerations For Communication That Supports A Continuous Blending Of Strategic Initiatives With Day-To-Day Operations

Guide and look for opportunities that make the most sense for a given individual's participation. Note that in chapter 11, I will explore individual-level communication and strategic initiative participation strategies as part of the organization's HR management and evaluation system.

Foster a communication structure that allows staff to embrace executive objectives, receive personal satisfaction out of success, obtain a feeling of achievement, and be a part of a group.

Focus the ongoing integrated communications structure toward the critical strategic issues and initiatives you are trying to address. Again, a successful communication structure supports the execution of strategy into operations that results in improved organizational performance. This communication structure is not meant to be confused with or to replace other mandatory or desired staff communication. As already described, it is meant to be an integrated blended strategic/operations communication structure that produces successful execution of executive objectives and enhanced organizational performance.

The continuous blending of strategic initiatives with a day-to-day operations structure is envisioned to support a multi-initiative environment and not just be oriented toward one-off initiatives.

As executives, do not lose sight of the fact that a major benefit to this structure and feedback loops is the ability to simultaneously address multiple organizational strategic executions focused on multiple objectives. In future chapters, I will describe in more detail this multi-initiative environment approach.

The communication structure should be viewed as consisting of a multilevel of communications simultaneously taking place, but still all focused on the blending of strategic and operational efforts.

Level one: These are the highest-level communications that lay the groundwork for the what and whys of the executive initiatives the organization will be embracing moving forward. They are intended for a more global audience.

The objective is to pave the way by informing the staff what will be happening and why, and to let them know there will be a need for their support and possible engagement. These communications provide an opportunity to create a global feedback loop where information is fed downwards to the staff as an introduction to the challenges and objectives of the organization while providing an opportunity to the staff for the upward flow of input and reaction.

In other words, it is the "heads-up" communication with an opportunity to receive "Have you thought about this?" or "Should there be a concern about that?" from the staff.

Level two: These communications are at the development, launch, and conclusion of a specific initiative or set of initiatives. They are oriented toward those areas and individuals in the organization most impacted by the initiative(s) and/or whose engagement in the initiative(s) is important. These communications can also be viewed as an initiation of the specific feedback loops for each given initiative.

Level three: These are the ground-level execution communications of a given initiative. They represent a continuous feedback loop regarding the monitoring and control of the status, assumptions, and conditions related to a specific initiative.

They define what the assumptions and critical factors are, why and how to monitor the actual conditions against these assumptions and factors, who should perform the monitoring, and when and how this information will be communicated upward in the organization.

As you can see, this multilevel set of communications supports the simultaneous execution of multiple initiatives.

While care must be given to workload balance and the potential for strategic initiative overload, a successful blending of the execution of strategic initiatives with day-to-day operations assumes some level of simultaneous strategic executions.

In conclusion, the following is an example of what a set of level-two communications might look like.

Example: Communication At The Launch Of An Initiative

"We believe our competitors have a lower cost structure, increasing their market share compared to ours.

"To make ourselves more competitive and increase market share, we have a series of ongoing initiatives we are launching that we expect will increase our throughput by 20 percent.

"The first initiative will be the introduction of a new process.

"While the implementation will require participation throughout the organization, we recognize there might be some additional anxiety in department X, given that this is where the focus of many of these initial changes is taking place.

"With the help and input from many of you in this group, we believe we have developed a good action plan, but as always, while there might be limits to any adjustments we can make, we are looking forward to your feedback and any concerns you might have.

"As a part of this action plan, we have determined a set of critical factors that will need to be continuously monitored and will be soliciting your assistance in these efforts.

"Our goal is to start these initial efforts on August 10 and have the implementation completed in six weeks, at which time we will discuss follow-on efforts.

"As always, please let us know if you see any opportunities to shorten this time frame or improve the plan.

"We intend to provide everyone involved with continuous feedback on the progress of these efforts and will be requiring and appreciate your ongoing feedback and support."

Example: Communication At The Completion Of The Execution

"We have completed the project and have already experienced a 5 percent improvement in throughput.

"I want to thank everyone involved, especially department X and Sandra A., for helping us maintain our targeted launch date.

"I also want to thank Jim B. for the input that allowed us to improve the process we have implemented.

"Our next project to help improve our ability to compete with our competitors is expected to start on December 1.

"Once again, we are creating an action plan that includes critical factors that we will need to monitor.

"As a part of developing the action plan, we will be reaching out to some of you for your feedback and involvement.

"As always, your continuous support and feedback are greatly appreciated."

10

HR Management Methodology I
Categorization Of Organizational Positions

Illustration: I will never forget the economic downturn of 2008 and 2009.

It was obvious that things were going to become very challenging.

I remember holding a companywide meeting and asking how many people had ever experienced a recession.

Out of hundreds of staff, only one or so staff raised their hand.

Fortunately, because of my broad base of executive exposure both domestically and internationally, I had a lot of experience managing in some very diverse and challenging economic conditions.

While I cannot say our organization and staff never experienced anxiety and stress, I can say that I do believe, based upon my observations, compared to most organizations, the amount of anxiety and stress was minimized, and the company exited the challenges of 2008 and 2009 a stronger organization. In fact, one of the most profitable years ever for the organization was 2009.

In today's world, human resource management has grown in significance and attention but is still an area in which the executive encounters many challenges.

Challenges associated with periods of excess and/or lack of worker availability, recessions, inflation, compensation equality and transparency, productivity, effects of technology and automation, and proper training techniques have challenged executive management for a long time.

The problem is not that the dynamics we are experiencing are new.

The problem is that the training executives are provided and the advice they receive from experts in human resource management is generally inadequate and fails their needs.

Compliance in human resources is always important. However, what follows are concepts that allow the executive to approach human resource management with tools that support a pragmatic strategic focus versus strictly an operational compliant-dominated perspective.

The systems and approaches that Dynamic Execution introduces are easy to implement and execute, and are industry agnostic, so it can be applied to any type of organization.

As previously discussed, these concepts, tools, and methodologies are derived from my years of executive experience in managing human resources across diverse environments—both domestically and internationally. This experience includes navigating periods of inflation, recession, varying unemployment levels, and working with both union and nonunion staff.

Flexible And Responsive

The first thing we need to recognize is that we require a methodology that is flexible and can be responsive and effective under multiple conditions and environments.

For example, in figures 10.1 through 10.3, I look at just the three variables of unemployment, Gross Domestic Product (GDP), and inflation historically.[8]

Figure 10.1

Economic Assumptions

Acceptable Range Assumptions	
Variable	**Assumed Acceptable Range**
Unemployment (Year-End)	4 percent to 6 percent
GDP (Annual)	1 percent to 3 percent
Inflation (Year-Over-Year)	0 percent to 2 percent

Figure 10.2

Economic Occurrences 1970 To 2019

Yearly Occurrences 1970 To 2019 (50 Years) And 2000 To 2019 (20 Years)						
Period	**Unemployment**		**GDP**		**Inflation**	
	Number Of Years Less Than 4 Percent	Number Of Years Greater Than 6 Percent	Number Of Years Less Than 1 Percent	Number Of Years Greater Than 3 Percent	Number Of Years Less Than 0 Percent	Number Of Years Greater Than 2 Percent
50 Years (1970–2019)	4	22	9	23	0	38
20 Years (2000–2019)	3	6	3	3	0	11

Figure 10.3

Economic Environments Twenty-Year Summary By Conditions

TWENTY-Year Summary		Number Of Years Of Occurrence	% Of Total Years
Acceptable Conditions	2003, 2014, and 2015	3	15%
Unemployment <= 4% Only	2018	1	5%
Unemployment > 6% Only	2010, 2012, and 2013	3	15%
GDP <= 1% Only	2001	1	5%
Inflation > 2% Only	2002, 2006, 2007, 2016, and 2017	5	25%
GDP > 3% And Inflation >2%	2004 and 2005	2	10%
Unemployment > 6% And GDP <= 1%	2008	1	5%
Unemployment > 6% And Inflation >2%	2011	1	5%
Unemployment > 6% And GDP <=1% And Inflation >2%	2009	1	5%
Unemployment <= 4% And Inflation >= 2%	2019	1	5%
Unemployment <= 4% And GDP > 3% And Inflation >2%	2000	1	5%
Twenty Years (2000–2019)		20	100%

These figures indicate how organizations have been operating under constantly changing economic conditions from a HR management perspective.

The twenty-year summary in figure 10.3 demonstrates that in just the twenty years from 2000 through 2019, organizations have had to adapt and contend with the dynamics of eleven different conditional environments, over multiple periods, when just considering the factors of unemployment rates, GDP, and inflation rates.

These are just three factors and do not account for other important considerations, such as changing federal and state regulations, financial and profitability concerns, market disruptors like social media and pandemics, evolving technology, compensation transparency, shifting work-life balances, and the dynamics of remote work.

What I will present here are innovative tools, techniques, and approaches for human resource management that executives can employ that will not only be successful across constantly changing dynamics, but also represent a systematic approach to staff hiring, retention, and compensation; staff evaluations; productivity improvements; organizational strategic execution; and organizational staff communications, increasing both consistency and efficiency.

Characteristics of these innovative approaches provide the executive with a comprehensive strengths and weaknesses profile of *both* strategic and operational execution capabilities within the organization down to the individual level. This profile includes a strategic focus versus just an operational compliance focus with communication and integration of strategic initiatives down to the individual level.

It also incorporates organizational, departmental, and functional considerations and is instrumental in organizational, departmental, and functional strategic planning and execution.

In addition, it has the advantage of being extremely responsive to analyzing changing environmental conditions and supporting response planning from a human resource management perspective while supporting organizational objectives. It recognizes, delineates, and differentiates position and staff significance levels within a given organization, department, and functional area. It also provides standardized, consistent, and repeatable tools for staff compensation, evaluations, goal setting, and staff communications.

Steps: New Innovative Human Resource Management Tools, Techniques, And Approaches

Step one categorizes each position in the organization. Categorization is based on the significance to the fundamental existence and survival of the organization and the significance to strategic execution and day-to-day operations.

In many cases, factors such as skill set requirements, time to train, ability to backfill the duties, and availability of qualified individuals might be applied to categorization when determining significance. *However, this is strictly a focus on the position, and specific individuals should not be taken into consideration in the categorization.*

Step two creates an assessment methodology that is applied to all individuals in the organization. As examined in more detail in chapter 11, this assessment goes beyond traditional performance measurements to include important organizational factors of (a) contribution to strategic initiative execution and productivity improvements, (b) contribution to innovation, (c) level of cross-training, (d) capability to support organizational change such as major growth and/or an organizational rebound, and (e) personal feedback such as areas of interest and willingness to participate.

In step three a human resource organizational assessment summary is created. The human resource assessment summary depicts both the positional categorization and individual assessments in a format that will support the analysis required for determining human resource strategies and human resource planning. Chapter 11 provides examples of such a human resource assessment summary.

Finally, in step four, this new human resource categorization, evaluation, and analysis methodology is incorporated into organizational strategic planning, day-to-day operations, and overall human resource management, including compensation programs, goal setting, and staff communications.

Step One: Categorize Each Position In The Organization

This new human resource categorization, evaluation, and analysis methodology begins with categorizing positions within an organization based on the specific level of significance represented by that position. Every position in an organization is reviewed from an organizational perspective, a departmental perspective, and a functional perspective.

Figure 10.4 details the structural nature and provides examples of what the different types of positional categorizations that can exist within an organization might look like. A basic categorization could include Critical, Essential, Required-Stable, Required-Flexible, or Part-Time/Temporary. Figure 10.4 also provides a definition of the different categories of importance to an organization and highlights the where and why behind these different categories. These classifications and definitions can be tailored to an organization's specific context and needs.

Positional categorization analysis is not intended to be complicated or burdensome to maintain. In order to keep it simple, I suggest creating an organization chart that includes both current and potential positions along with a brief description of activities and responsibilities. Also, indicate the significance/categorization of each position. Please note individuals are not named, only the position.

The creation of these charts should start with middle management's (Sr. Managers/Directors) positional assessment of the responsibilities under their control down to departmental/functional level positions. This output is then reviewed, signed off, and built upon moving upward in the organization. This forces the organization to analyze and document which positions are most vital and why.

Positional categorization is a thought generation tool that produces a structured analytical capability the C-suite can use to help quickly assess strengths, exposures, priorities, and critical requirements from a structural human resource perspective. This information represents a well-thought-out basis that can be utilized for everything from exposure analysis to establishing staff evaluation criteria, compensation considerations, and staffing for both strategic and operational planning.

The categorization provides a method of analyzing both current and future critical organization human resource requirements not only for operational success but for alignment with executive strategic direction and accomplishment of objectives. In addition, it provides another level of guidance when faced with determining staffing and resource priorities and structures during periods of growth, rationalization, or responses to changing external and internal dynamics.

Because it is agnostic and position-focused only, it is unencumbered from a focus on specific individuals and instead is focused strictly on the critical activities required for success. For example, critical and essential positions would almost always be priorities when there is an allocation of limited resources or in times of major organizational structural changes. The focus would first be on the support of these critical and essential activities and only then be on specific individuals that represent the best alternatives to fill those positions.

Therefore, an up-front discussion and creation of these activity-based priorities through positional categorizations will, when needed, immediately provide an existing analytical basis to make tough decisions. This helps avoid what I have more often than not seen as on-the-fly, disjointed, and unstructured analytical justifications and attempts at staff priority setting and decision-making.

As executives, it is important to remember that, in times of need (often in times of stress), discussions of these sorts of positional and staffing priorities are going to take place either consciously or unconsciously and are either structured or unstructured. Therefore, all I am promoting here is to do it in advance, consciously, and in a structured context. This will not only provide an existing analytical basis when needed but also provide you with an ongoing tool to continually plan and control your critical human resources.

While there can be classificatory overlap among various organizations, the categorical classification of positions can and will vary significantly among organizations based upon such factors as the type of organization (i.e., manufacturing versus service versus governmental versus nonprofit), size, public versus private, placement on company life cycle, industry, market, location, etc.

While some might find the concept of assigning significance to a position potentially concerning, please note the following.

The categorization is associated specifically with the *position* and the relevance that position has to the success of the organization, department, or functional area. While different positions might represent different levels of availability, specialty, training, and skill sets, from the perspective of the individual, it is agnostic.

Therefore, it assumes that anyone with the proper training, skill set, and qualifications can be appropriate for the position. Because it is agnostic, it is assumed that no issues should be created from a human resource compliance perspective.

The strength of the methodology recognizes and supports that an established categorization can be specific to each organization. For example, a critical position in a hospital might be a specific type of doctor, while a critical position in an automotive service center might be a specific type of mechanic. Again, both are equally significant, and this significance and importance are based upon only the qualifications and dynamics associated with that specific position to the organization, department, and functional area.

Positional categorizations for a given organization can and will vary over time. What is critical or important today can change significantly as the dynamics within and outside of the organization change. For example, an essential position during product development might be an engineer or product manager position, and then it might shift to an essential position of a marketing manager position when the product is due to launch. That is what makes this methodology so powerful; it helps an organization more effectively plan in advance and react to these changing conditions.

The next chapter will continue the discussion of the innovative concepts associated with the human resource categorization, evaluation, and analysis methodology by exploring the evaluation and analysis portions of these new approaches.

Figure 10.4

Structural Nature And Examples Of Positional Categorizations

Category Description	Definition	Where/Why Used	Examples
Critical Category	Positions that are critical to the fundamental existence and survival of the organization. These can be viewed as an organization's heart-and-soul positions or positions critical to the organization's underlying ability to function and exist.	Used only at the organizational level since the significance crosses all departmental, functional, and hierarchical considerations. A definition and understanding of these positions are critical relative to compensation planning and in times of growth, reorganizations, and downsizing.	• Heavily Regulated Industry Compliance Officer • Highly Engineered Products VP Of Engineering • Large Consumer Products VP Of Marketing • Major Bank Risk Officer • Publicly Traded CFO • PaaS Service Provider Chief Technology Officer
Essential Category	Positions that are essential to maintaining effective and efficient day-to-day operations at the organization. The organization will experience major disruptions or difficulties if these positions fail to execute their duties effectively and efficiently. Need to focus on the specific position and not general positional descriptions. For example, just because you have a specific manager position as essential does not mean all manager positions should be considered essential.	Used at the departmental and functional levels. Unless a departmental or functional position has already been classified as organizationally critical, it can be categorized as essential. A definition and understanding of these positions are critical relative to compensation planning and in times of growth, reorganizations, and downsizing.	• Medical Devices Quality Control Technician • Publicly Traded Director Of Internal Controls • Largest Customer Sales And/Or Customer Support Rep • Certified Products Test Cell Operator • Multinational Corporate Treasurer • Nonprofit Director Of Fundraising • Warehousing And Transportation Logistics Manager • High-End Restaurant Chef • Software Applications Director Of Software Development

Category Description	Definition	Where/Why Used	Examples
Required-Stable Category	Positions that are required for day-to-day operations and where stability of the staffing is important due to skill set, training, or other operational considerations. Skill set requirements, time to train, ability to backfill the duties, and availability of qualified individuals internally and externally are major differentiators between required-stable and required-flexible. Need to focus on the specific position and not general positional descriptions. For example, just because a specific type of maintenance specialist position is required-stable does not mean all maintenance positions should be considered required-stable. Therefore, these maintenance positions can be a mixture of essential, required-stable, required-flexible, or even temporary.	Used at the departmental and functional levels. Unless a departmental or functional position has already been classified as organizationally critical or departmentally and/or functionally essential, it can be categorized as required-stable. Failure to adequately staff these positions over time can cause disruptions and difficulties at a departmental or function level. A definition and understanding of these positions are important relative to compensation planning and in times of growth, reorganizations, and downsizing.	· Production Line Supervisor · Accounts Payable Processor · Design Engineer · IT Programmer · Quality Control Technician · Sales Representative · Benefits Administrator · Automotive Mechanic · Maintenance Specialist · Truck Driver · Hospitality Or Food And Beverage Manager · Department Manager · Installation Technician · Equipment Repair Specialist

Category Description	Definition	Where/Why Used	Examples
Required-Flexible Category	Positions that are required for day-to-day operations where stability of the staffing might be preferred, but flexibility of staffing is available due to the ability to backfill or augment these duties. Skill set requirements, time to train, ability to backfill the duties, and availability of qualified individuals internally and externally are major differentiators between required-stable and required-flexible.	Used at the departmental and functional levels. Unless a departmental or functional position has already been classified as organizationally critical or departmentally and/or functionally essential or required-stable, it can be categorized as required-flexible. The nature of the duties for these positions are such that alternatives are readily available and/or failure to timely execute represents limited exposure to the organization.	• Forklift Driver • Assembly-Line Worker • Administrative Clerical • Packaging Clerk • Bartender • Server Staff • Cashier • Data Entry • Housekeeping
Temporary/ Part-Time (Short Or Long Term)	Positions that are temporary and that are either filled with full-time staff who will be reassigned after completion of the assignment, who are part-time, or are temporary staff hires. These are also often filled with contract labor.	Used at the departmental and functional levels of the organization. Should be defined as temporary but also can be cobranded as critical, essential, or required if the assignment is deemed as such.	• Programmer • Network Support Technician • Barista • Marketing Coordinator • Website Developer • Social Media Coordinator • Server Staff • Delivery Driver • Systems Design Specialist

11

HR Management Methodology II
Staff Evaluations And
HR Resource Analysis Capabilities

In chapter 10, I provided an introduction to Dynamic Execution's innovative tools, techniques, and approaches to the management of an organization's human resources. I concluded with a discussion of step one: the categorization of the significance relative to each position existing within an organization.

This chapter will now explore the remaining steps starting with step two, the establishment of a broadened individual staff-level evaluation structure.

However, before we continue, I want to revisit the illustration I presented at the beginning of chapter 10.

Illustration: I ended my illustration in chapter 10 by indicating that even though there were major economic challenges occurring in 2008 and 2009, the organization was not only profitable during that period of time but exited stronger than ever before.

Following the concepts and tools I describe in chapters 8 through 11, strong communication and feedback channels were available that kept the staff continuously aware of the dynamics taking place and solicited their input and participation on critical issues.

Operational and staff restructuring were executed following the human resource methodology processes outlined here and were based upon analysis focused on critical positions and staff assessments.

It was understood up front that, at some point, the negative economic dynamics taking place would start to change/improve.

Therefore, it was important to prioritize the retention of critical positions, maintain the staff who had the best cross-training for current operations, and maintain the staff with the best knowledge and capability required to efficiently and effectively support future operational requirements when the economic dynamics improved.

This was unlike many organizations that followed the accountants and experts down a path of focusing on cost-downs based on compensation levels and, many times, arbitrary criteria. In fact, every effort was made to maintain as much as possible existing compensation expectations and even, in some cases, increase the compensation levels for the staff involved in critical positions.

We continued the execution of critical strategic executions through a blended organizational structure that allowed the organization to exit the downturn much more operationally efficient and productive.

Step Two: Establish A Comprehensive Individual Assessment Structure

Once you have categorized all the positions within your organization, this innovative human-resource methodology shifts the focus to actual individual assessments within each of those positions.

The categorization of the positions within the methodology outlines and assists in analyzing where you need to focus your resources and attention. The personnel assessment focuses on the evaluation of the strengths and challenges associated with actual individuals assigned to each position.

However, this innovative methodology requires the assessment of individuals to extend well beyond the evaluation of just performance in a particular position. It requires that a broader perspective is taken so that it is easier to analyze and assess alternatives during times of changing dynamics.

The objective is not to replace the basic evaluation of skill set and performance but to extend the evaluations to include an individual's level of cross-training, contribution or potential contribution to strategic initiative execution and productivity improvements, contribution or potential contribution to innovation, capability to support organizational change, such as major growth and/or an organizational rebound, and personal feedback, such as areas of interest and willingness to participate.

This expanded assessment criteria extends the capability of the executive and the organization to determine strengths, weaknesses, exposures, and opportunities all the way down to the level of the individual contributor.

In addition, as described in the above illustration, it provides invaluable guidance when making decisions regarding staffing during times of growth, rationalizing, strategic execution, or in response to any other number of changing environmental dynamics.

Finally, this assessment methodology supports the utilization of executive-to-individual communication and feedback loops.

The table in figure 11.1 provides details of the individual assessment criteria, including the extended criteria.

When viewed in totality, figure 11.1 represents a much more holistic and integrated perspective of the staff within an organization—a perspective that can provide an executive with powerful, straightforward, and easy-to-apply information when addressing tough internal and external organizational challenges.

Figure 11.1

Description Of Individual Staff Assessment Criteria

Assessment Description	Definition	Why	Discussion
Skill Set	How the individual's skill set matches the skill set requirements of the position.	It is important to understand at both the organizational and individual level how comprehensive and proficient the skill sets are at each position. This is especially important when assessing capabilities for the critical and essential positions.	This assessment not only helps to evaluate the potential strengths and weakness in the organization at various positional categories, but is a great tool to communicate areas of an individual's strengths and help set goals and action plans for areas an individual can improve. Skill set can also be a differentiator when determining and justifying compensation and paths for advancement.

Assessment Description	Definition	Why	Discussion
Performance	This is how well the individual applies their skills to accomplish the required tasks of the position. This should be a very open dialogue and should also take into consideration the upstream and downstream positional performance ramifications.	Even if an individual has the necessary skill set, their actual performance may exceed or fail to meet the execution and accomplishment of the required objectives, goals, and tasks of a position. These assessments can provide an excellent opportunity to make sure the required objectives, goals, and tasks of a position have been clearly defined, understood by all parties, and communicated. It also provides an opportunity to assess the possible existence of shortfalls and opportunities for improvements.	The evaluation and review of performance is a great tool to communicate areas of an individual's strengths and to help set goals and action plans for areas an individual can improve. It also represents an ideal opportunity to explore areas for organizational improvements and communicate and solicit feedback regarding new organizational, departmental, or functional initiatives. Performance can also be a differentiator when determining and justifying compensation and paths for advancement.
Adherence To And Knowledge Of Safety Protocols	Determine the level of knowledge, understanding, and adherence to organizational safety protocols. Solicit feedback, suggestions, and concerns to assist in the analysis and improvement of the protocols.	An organization's focus on safety should always be a major criterion. Many would argue that safety should be the first organizational priority followed by quality of product/service and delivery/customer satisfaction, especially given many of the dynamics that exist in today's environment. Therefore, assessing and training individuals on existing safety protocols and soliciting their input and feedback is a critical criterion in the assessment process.	The main objective of this portion of the assessment is to make sure the safety protocols are communicated, understood, and adhered to. This also opens the communication lines for an individual's input including feedback, suggestions, and concerns.

Assessment Description	Definition	Why	Discussion
New Level Of Cross-Training	How much cross-training an individual has. Care must be given that cross-training is not limited to only different positions but also includes cross-training in various skill sets within a given positional category. For example, there could be a single position defined as production line assembly. However, there might be multiple stations along the production line that require different skill sets and, therefore, represent cross-training opportunities for both the individual and organization. Another example might be a position defined as design engineer, which includes a base skill set in a specific release of design software. However, if an individual broadens their skill set to include different release levels of that software or bolt-on packages to that software, this would also be considered cross-training given the position of design engineer has not changed and the individual's skill set exceeds the basic skill set defined for that position.	Cross-trained individuals in multiple positions and/or skill sets represent an increased value proposition to the organization. Therefore, not only should this cross-training be recognized and defined at the individual level but cross-training structures and planning should be established by the organization. The goal should be to focus on opportunities to: · Reduce operational disruptions · Improve efficiency, effectiveness, productivity, and training · Provide opportunities for an individual's growth and advancement · Determine who the critical resources are in times of growth, reorganization, or rebounding	The level and amount of an individual's cross-training can be a big differentiator when: · Determining and justifying compensation · Determining which individuals are retained at times of downsizing, like during recessionary periods · Determining paths for an individual's growth and advancement Cross-training compensation matrixes can be a useful tool and should be utilized when deemed appropriate.

Assessment Description	Definition	Why	Discussion
New Capability To Support Organizational Growth And/Or An Organizational Rebounding	This assessment defines which capabilities an individual possesses that can be applied and leveraged by an organization during periods of rapid growth, reorganization, or most importantly, when an organization is in a downturn and ultimately rebounding from that downturn (for example, during and after downsizing due to a recession). These capabilities go beyond the level of an individual's cross-training and must include an evaluation of an individual's: • Ability to train others • Ability and flexibility to backfill other positions or skill sets • Possession of strong organizational knowledge and operational know-how • Most important, a willingness to accept additional workload as needed and train or retrain individuals as the organization rebounds or grows	This is one of the most unidentified and underutilized capabilities in an organization. Yet in times of unexpected or undeterminable growth, or in times of restructuring or downsizing due to changing market conditions or economic conditions such as a recession, individuals with these capabilities prove to be invaluable. Unfortunately, individuals with these capabilities along with individuals filling critical and essential positions within the organization are too often swept up in times of restructuring and layoffs. This is especially the case when the criteria used is predominantly based upon compensation levels. Ironically, retaining and utilizing individuals with these capabilities can create a significant amount of cost savings, allow the organization to rebound more quickly, and provide the best continuity of organizational knowledge and operational know-how.	These capabilities are most utilized during periods of: • unexpected growth • undeterminable growth such as an inability to predict demand that will be generated from the launch of a customer's product • an organizational restructuring • downsizing due to changing market conditions or economic conditions such as a recession Therefore, an individual's capabilities in this area will be a differentiator when: • Determining and justifying compensation • Determining which individuals are retained at times of organizational restructuring or downsizing (like during recessionary periods) • Determining paths for an individual's growth and advancement

Assessment Description	Definition	Why	Discussion
New **Contribution To Strategic Initiative Execution And Productivity Improvements**	This evaluation brings the contributions to strategic initiative execution and productivity improvements to the grassroots level. When assessing an individual's contributions (including potential contributions), the organization should not only focus on ideas/suggestions for improvements, but just as importantly, on an individual's involvement in and support of the execution of strategic and productivity improvement initiatives. Many a great initiative failed to reach full potential or even completely failed due to a lack of participation, support, input, and desire at the individual level. Leadership must recognize that participation can be required at every position in the organization for productivity improvement and strategic initiative opportunities. Therefore, an assessment of an individual's involvement or potential involvement is critical.	Much is written regarding strategic execution and productivity improvement including an endless number of "how-to" strategies, methodologies, and incentive systems. However, including this evaluation criteria in an individual's assessment across all staff places a higher level of significance to these efforts. It also provides greater flexibility in motivating, recognizing, and incentivizing individuals to participate in the development and/ or execution of strategic initiatives and productivity improvements. Through this assessment, the organization receives a significant benefit from the knowledge associated with which positions and which individuals are important and are contributors to these efforts. The use of this assessment criteria enhances the ability to communicate important organizational initiatives and solicit the input, creativity, acceptance, and participation required from an individual to support feedback loops.	An individual's contributions and potential contributions to strategic initiative execution and productivity improvement can be a big differentiator when: • Determining and justifying compensation • Determining which individuals are retained at times of downsizing, like during recessionary periods • Determining paths for an individual's growth and advancement This process is consistent with the objective of blending strategic initiatives with day-to-day operations by communicating down details of important organizational initiatives and soliciting up the input, creativity, acceptance, and participation of individuals in strategic execution and productivity improvement efforts. It is base level communication and participation in feedback loops.

Assessment Description	Definition	Why	Discussion
New **Contribution To Innovation**	Evaluation of contributions to innovation has a different focus from evaluation of contributions to strategic initiatives and productivity improvements. Innovation represents contributions to major advancements, and smaller positive operational impacts through the creation and/or involvement in innovative tools, methods, and solutions that address often unrecognized problems or opportunities. This includes such things as unique devices or methods that provide solutions where no other known solution exits, contributions that significantly enhances product and service offerings or unique operating systems and structures. Recognition of innovative contribution within the assessment process can be far more effective than any sort of staff suggestion or other type of staff idea solicitation/appreciation program.	There are major motivational, communications, and recognition benefits in developing a deeper understanding and recognition of staff who represent contributors, or potential contributors, to innovation. Key factors to consider: · Generally, applies to a more limited number of staff and are often considered go-to problem solvers · Assessments focus on the creative and innovative activities of staff who have positive operational impacts that might not otherwise be adequately recognized or reinforced and represents effort that goes beyond normal responsibilities · Can apply to staff at any level in the organization including staff assigned to normal innovation activities (for example R&D) when their activities go beyond expected skill set and performance activities	Represents superior motivational, communication, and acknowledgment benefits than traditional staff suggestion programs or other systems for soliciting staff recommendations and involvement. Goes beyond skill set and can represent a differentiator for: · Determining and justifying compensation · Determining which individuals are retained at times of downsizing like during recessionary periods · Determining paths for an individual's growth and advancement

Assessment Description	Definition	Why	Discussion
New Input From The Individual	This assessment criteria explores the individual's level of satisfaction, areas of interest, desired growth paths if any, concerns, and willingness to be cross-trained or take on additional responsibilities.	These can be viewed by many as difficult conversations but in fact represent a great opportunity to: · Coordinate an individual's desires and expectations with organizational needs and priorities · Establish individual goals and action plans · Provide open dialogue · Communicate organizational goals and direction, and impacts these might have on the individual · Communicate how the individual's compensation has been determined and if there are any action plans that might influence future considerations · Explore possible unknown capabilities, ideas, or desires and willingness to participate in other organizational opportunities that they might be qualified for	This should be applied as an open communication tool that can be used to: · Explore what the individual's desires, ideas, and concerns are · Explain the compensation criteria that was used and possible opportunities to influence the level of future compensation · Look for and establish specific action plans · Communicate organizational opportunities and explore possible participation · Communicate current organizational goals and objective · Assess the individual's level of satisfaction and willingness to expand their skill sets or participate in new opportunities · Determine if the individual has any unknown applicable skill sets or capabilities that should be taken into consideration

Strategic Versus Operational Staff Assessment Criteria

It is important at this point to make the following observations regarding assessments.

I often receive a reaction, especially from human resource professionals, of "This appears logically sound and beneficial, but who is going to perform and control this analysis? It is already difficult to get timely and comprehensive evaluations completed." Having personally observed and experienced this dynamic, I have a great deal of empathy for this reaction.

However, this book focuses on tools to improve the C-suite's ability to accomplish objectives, not general management techniques or human resource management. The reality is that, from a C-suite perspective, the evaluation of skill sets and performance criteria should be viewed as having an operationally oriented focus.

However, the focus of the new evaluation criteria I am presenting is on important strategic, executive-oriented data such as contribution to strategic initiative execution and productivity improvements, contribution to innovation, the levels of cross-training that exists within the organization, capability to support organizational change, and an individual staff's personal feedback such as areas of interest and willingness to participate. In other words, these evaluation criteria assess the organization's capability to support strategic execution and obtain desired objectives.

This strategic focus means the primary responsibility to know, accumulate, analyze, and understand this information resides with middle management (again, senior managers/directors) and moves up into the organizational hierarchy from there. This is one of the reasons I discussed early on in the book that strategic versus operational activities within an organization are generally underestimated, misunderstood, and represent a missed opportunity for executives to improve the execution of their objectives.

One could argue that there are other pathways that can be used to accumulate this information. And I would agree the accumulation and availability of this data has inherent significant importance independent of how it is obtained. However, by incorporating this exercise into an individual's assessment process, you gain the ability to have direct communication of strategic information, activities, and bidirectional feedback at the lowest level possible, the individual.

From a strategic standpoint, a major benefit of using these human resource categorization, evaluation, and analytical tools is that they provide a structure to analyze which positions and which specific staff are the most vital human resources to the organization during any given period of time or set of conditions. And maybe even more importantly, it provides an indication of where the organization has exposure and requires additional training or focus on improvements in staffing.

In turn, this provides a basis and logic behind the strategic planning of staff compensation and retention. For example, this means that, with everything being equal, you should rarely, if ever, lose the most comprehensively and positively assessed staff members since they represent the most valuable human resources to the organization. This is especially true of positively assessed staff in critical and essential positions.

If, through an adjustment to compensation or other variables, you find your organization attempting to retain an individual after learning of the individual's intention to leave, this is a clear indication that the organization is not doing something correctly in the evaluation and management of strategically critical resources.

Step Three: Create A Human Resource Organizational Assessment Summary

Assessment summaries are intended to accumulate staff data at the lowest denominator—the individual.

They should include all pertinent data that will allow for comprehensive analysis and sorting.

Figure 11.2 is a table of a sample template of the *Spreadsheet Columns* that should be included in an assessment summary.

Figure 11.2

Sample Spreadsheet *Column* Template For Individual Staff Assessment Summary

Description Of Assessment To Be Performed	Description Of Assessment Criteria	Spreadsheet Column Reference
Date	Date of the assessment	A
Position Description	Description of position for the individual being assessed	B
Name Of Individual Assigned	Name of the individual being assessed	C
Department Or Functional Area	Department or functional area the assessed individual is assigned to	D
Skill Set	N/A or 1 To 5 rating individual is receiving (establish an action plan if applicable)	E
	Notation if an action plan is available (A=Action Plan In Place)	F
Performance	N/A or 1 To 5 rating individual is receiving (establish an action plan if applicable)	G
	Notation if an action plan is available (A=Action Plan In Place)	H
Adherence To And Knowledge Of Safety Protocols	G=Good T=Needs Training R=Issues To Be Resolved (action plan required if R)	I
NEW – Capability To Support Organizational Change	N/A or 1 To 5 **OVERALL** rating individual is receiving (establish an action plan if applicable)	J
	N/A or 1 To 5 **LEVEL OF CROSS TRAINING** rating individual is receiving (establish a cross-training matrix for individual if applicable)	K
	N/A or 1 To 5 **ABILITY TO TRAIN** rating individual is receiving (document specific areas of capability if applicable)	L
	N/A or 1 To 5 **ABILITY TO BACKFILL** rating individual is receiving (document specific areas of capability if applicable)	M
	N/A or 1 To 5 **ORGANIZATION AND/OR OPERATIONAL KNOWLEDGE** rating individual is receiving (document specific areas of capability if applicable)	N
	N/A or 1 To 5 **WILLINGNESS TO SUPPORT ORGANIZATION CHANGE ACTIVITIES** rating individual is receiving (document specific areas of capability and/or action plan if applicable)	O
	Notation if an action plan or other documented information is available (A=Documentation Available)	P

Description Of Assessment To Be Performed	Description Of Assessment Criteria	Spreadsheet Column Reference
NEW – Contribution To Strategic Initiatives And/Or Productivity Improvements	N/A or 1 To 5 **OVERALL** rating individual is receiving (establish an action plan if applicable)	Q
	N/A or 1 To 5 **IS A MAJOR INITIATOR** rating individual is receiving (document specifics if applicable)	R
	N/A or 1 To 5 **WILLINGNESS TO SUPPORT/PARTICIPATE IN ACTIVITIES** rating individual is receiving (document specifics if applicable)	S
	Notation if an action plan or other documented information is available (A=Documentation Available)	T
NEW – Contribution To Innovation	N/A or 1 To 5 **OVERALL** rating individual is receiving (establish an action plan if applicable)	U
	N/A or 1 To 5 **IS A MAJOR INITIATOR** rating individual is receiving (document specifics if applicable)	V
	N/A or 1 To 5 **WILLINGNESS TO SUPPORT/PARTICIPATE IN ACTIVITIES** rating individual is receiving (document specifics if applicable)	W
	Notation if an action plan or other documented information is available (A=Documentation Available)	X
NEW – Input From The Individual	ME=Meeting Staff Expectations SE=Short Of Staff Expectations (document staff expectations/concerns if SE)	Y
	Y or N if individual desires expanded responsibilities (document specifics and/or establish an action plan if applicable)	Z
	Y or N if individual has other skill sets available (document specifics and/or establish an action plan if applicable)	AA
	Other Comments (document specifics and/or establish an action plan if required)	AB
	Notation if an action plan or other documented information is available (A=Documentation Available)	AC

As depicted in this table, there are spreadsheet columns for typical assessment criteria such as skills and performance (columns E through I), but additional columns (columns J through AC) have been added to include the expanded assessment criteria introduced in figure 11.1 which are labeled as NEW in figure 11.2.

Using a spreadsheet that is formatted to include these figure 11.2 columns or a similar analytical data tool has some major benefits. It is easy, yet comprehensive, for the user to review and analyze. It can be sorted based on the specific criteria of interest and the analysis being performed.

Like the "Notation if an action plan is available" reference found in columns F and H, it can also easily be expanded if required to add columns that reference such things as available compensation schedules, specific productivity and innovation initiatives or to include columns to reference specific management.

In addition, it can be delineated and disbursed based on relevant data to individual departments, functional areas, initiatives, or managers and supervisors for ease of use, analysis, updating, and maintenance. It provides complete flexibility to adjust the format to meet the specific requirements at the organizational, departmental, and functional levels.

Note: The sample assessment summaries presented here only include columns for a numerical one through five rating. It should be recognized that there might be, and in most cases should be, a more detailed evaluation/feedback form associated with how a given rating was determined, along with including any notes of discussions and feedback received during the actual review with that individual.

It is apparent that each assessment will be individualized and based upon that staff's specific evaluations and feedback.

The assessment summary can easily be sorted into different configurations to further assist in the analysis of a particular area of interest. For example, if an organization is anticipating possible growth in a particular product offering, the assessment summary can be sorted by a specific department (column D) and then the capability to support organizational change (columns J through P) to determine which individuals have experience that can be leveraged or if instead, a weakness exists and the organization needs to focus attention on additional staff training or preparedness.

The assessment summary can also assist the human resource department in reviews, audits, and compliance verification. For example, they can verify that all the action plans included in the summary are available in the individual's file and that the summary accurately reflects all of the action plans the human resource department has in its possession.

Bottom line: The power of the human resource categorization, evaluation, and analysis methodology is not limited to only supplying an organization with a straightforward, cross-organizationally consistent set of processes. It also provides significant amounts of data for improved human resources management and planning.

Step Four: Incorporate The Innovative Human Resource Methodology Into Organizational Strategic Planning, Day-To-Day Operations, And Overall Human Resource Management

The prior discussions have provided you with numerous advantages and applications associated with these Dynamic Execution concepts, tools, and techniques. To summarize, we will break the benefits of using this methodology into four main categories.

Category 1: Strategic Analysis And Human Resource Planning

The ability for executives to quickly assess the strengths and weaknesses of the organization's human resources is significantly enhanced. The incorporation of the categorization of positions forces the organization to determine and come to a consensus as to what positions are truly critical and essential in the organization.

The expansion of evaluation criteria to include sections that evaluate (a) cross-training, (b) capability to support organizational change, (c) contribution to strategic initiative execution and productivity improvements, and (d) contribution to innovation provide executives new decision-making capabilities. This methodology expands the evaluation criteria to include strategically oriented factors that are not normally taken into consideration. This, in turn, provides an ability to determine the staff who have the greatest potential to influence success during periods of growth, restructuring, organizational rebounding (like when rebounding from the loss of a major customer or exiting a downturn or recessionary period), or when addressing other challenges associated with changing environmental conditions.

Finally, increased human resource data and analytical capability allow executives to improve decision-making in resource allocation, compensation structures, and staff recruitment and retention strategies and priorities.

Category 2: Day-To-Day Operational And Strategic Activities

The use of feedback loops supports the blending of strategic initiatives with day-to-day operations.

Operating and functional management receive new human resource tools, additional data, and a deeper understanding of the staff they are responsible for in areas such as training, productivity, innovation, and their capabilities and importance during periods of changing conditions. This, in turn, allows them to improve decision-making in (a) departmental or functional resource allocation, (b) compensation evaluations, (c) staff training and development, (d) staff retention strategies and priorities, (e) potential quality and efficiency performance enhancements, and (f) potential opportunities for productivity improvements.

In addition, these techniques improve staff relations. It provides individuals with (a) a deeper understanding of the processes and factors affecting their evaluation and compensation, (b) a deeper understanding of requirements and opportunities available for training, additional compensation, and advancement, and (c) increased opportunities to receive recognition, compensation, advancement, and job security. This is due to the fact that if an individual has the necessary capabilities and willingness, there is the potential for new opportunities due to the organization's expanded evaluation criteria.

Category 3: Human Resource Management And Compliance

These concepts, tools, and techniques provide the human resource department enhanced capabilities and departmental efficiencies by (a) utilizing a standardization methodology across the organization, (b) providing flexible, comprehensive, powerful analytical tools such as the human resource assessment summary, (c) providing an ability to distribute workload and effort while maintaining an appropriate level of control, and (d) providing additional enhanced staff data.

These capabilities, in turn, provide an improved ability to monitor, control, review, and analyze individual evaluation and compensation processes, along with enhanced recruitment processes through a deeper understanding of staffing priorities and an expanded knowledge of the basic and opportunistic criteria associated with each position.

In addition, there is improved development, monitoring, control, and evaluation of staff training and development programs, as well as individual action plans, improved efficiency, and effort associated with compliance verification and audits, and expanded opportunities for new and enhanced staff communication.

Category 4: Staff Communications And Involvement

The more subtle but powerful characteristics of these Dynamic Execution approaches to HR management are improved staff communication, improved staff feedback, improved staff participation, and motivated staff involvement.

The methodology provides an effective way of communicating what is going on within the organization in a relatable context. The organization improves staff communication of potential opportunities and improves the individual's knowledge of what is occurring that might directly or indirectly affect them. It also provides an opportunity for feedback and concerns from an individual regarding a specific initiative or direction.

The inclusion in the evaluation of an individual's personal feedback adds a significant tool for understanding their willingness to participate, areas of interest, unknown skill sets, and thoughts and concerns (including an ability to address any potential anxiety that exists). It solicits the individual's evaluation of the organization's ability to meet or not meet their job expectations and provides the opportunity to explore action plans that might improve the situation.

This new dialogue can lead to increasing an individual's involvement, improving an individual's support and cooperation for organizational objectives, uncovering possible risks and concerns associated with specific initiatives, improving staff satisfaction and retention, and addressing any misconceptions or inaccuracies that the individual might have.

The ability to increase staff motivation and involvement is accomplished due to the expanded set of evaluation criteria. Discussions are not strictly focused on skill sets and performance criteria. They will now include interactive dialogue regarding cross-training, level of organizational and operational knowledge, participation in strategic initiative executions, productivity improvements, and innovation initiatives. Therefore, the methodology communicates that participation, even supportive participation, in any of these areas can have a favorable impact on compensation, advancement, and security. For many, this generates motivation to get involved.

The power of the Dynamic Execution human resource framework and approaches for the executive cannot be overstated. It is comprehensive yet straightforward to execute and administer. It allows executives to quickly and easily assess the health, strengths, and challenges associated with one of the most important organizational resources, human resources.

Finally, here are concepts, tools, and techniques that provide the executive and the organization with the data and capabilities necessary for improved strategic planning, decision-making, and deep analysis of complicated issues to address an ever-changing environment.

PART IV

Dynamic Execution Foundational Pillar

Operational And Financial Validation

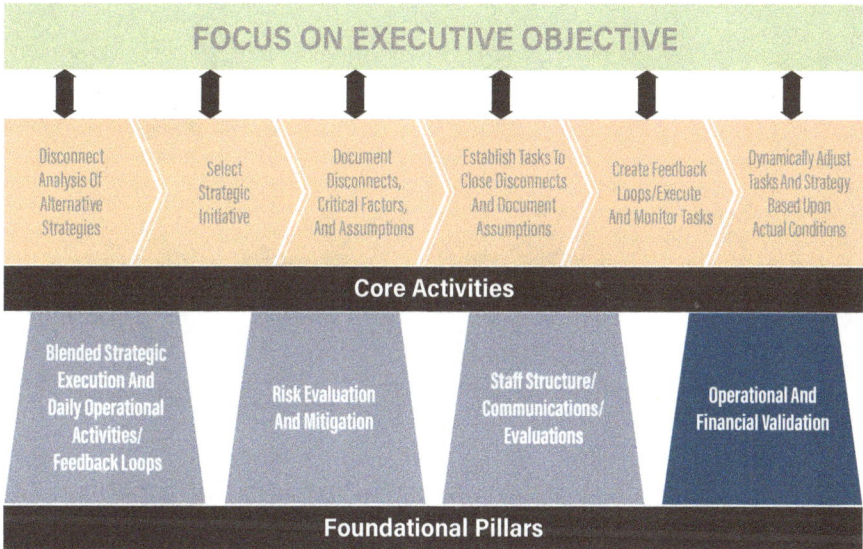

FOCUS ON EXECUTIVE OBJECTIVE

| Disconnect Analysis Of Alternative Strategies | Select Strategic Initiative | Document Disconnects, Critical Factors, And Assumptions | Establish Tasks To Close Disconnects And Document Assumptions | Create Feedback Loops/Execute And Monitor Tasks | Dynamically Adjust Tasks And Strategy Based Upon Actual Conditions |

Core Activities

| Blended Strategic Execution And Daily Operational Activities/Feedback Loops | Risk Evaluation And Mitigation | Staff Structure/Communications/Evaluations | Operational And Financial Validation |

Foundational Pillars

Chapter 12 details the importance and approach to the integration of finance and operations to continuously validate strategic objective expectations.

12

Beyond Budgeting
Operational And Financial Validation

Illustration: There was an experience I had that forever influenced my approach to strategic selection and execution.

I was an executive at a large company that had two main product lines.

While each represented a unique and different market, each required the same raw material and production resources.

Product line A had a higher price point with overall demand that was higher than product line B but insufficient to consume all of the available capacity.

Product line B had a lower price point but a higher yield on the use of the raw material. It also was seasonal but with a reliable demand.

The owner and senior executive management of the company established an objective of increasing sales and improving margins/profitability through increased capacity utilization. Of course, the allocation of both raw materials and production capacity between the two product lines became a strategic focal point.

Both product lines had somewhat consistent historical allocations creating strong, well-established, long-term advocates, making the selection of the strategy difficult.

Therefore, each group of advocates provided their own projections of demand, pricing, and resource requirements required to increase demand, leading to increased sales and profitability.

As the assumptions provided had credibility from a historical perspective, a strategic allocation of resources was made with the expectation of reaching the objectives.

Being involved from *both* an operational and financial context, I struggled with executing a strategy strictly based on assumptions and expectations using historical financial and operational data. Therefore, to validate the strategy selected, I created a financial model based on the assumptions and expectations used in the strategy.

To everyone's surprise, and many a displeasure, the model indicated that while the original strategy would yield an increase in sales and profitability, an allocation of 100 percent of the resources to product line A would yield a considerably greater increase in profitability. This was the case even if there were pricing concessions in product line A in order to fill capacity. This was due to the fact that the favorable pricing differential between product line A versus product line B was so large that it more than offset the favorable yield of product line B.

The company went on to test these new assumptions and strategies, not only verifying if they were correct but also that the break-even points between pricing and yields could then be used to solicit an increase in demand for product line A.

In the end, the company completely exited product line B and utilized all the production capacity through increased demand for product line A based upon the relationship of yield to pricing.

In addition, an ongoing integrated relationship was established between daily operations and financial modeling that continually monitored actual-to-assumed conditions. This integrated operations with financial structure yielded a capability to continually fine-tune the system even further, thereby creating an ability to significantly improve operational efficiency and overall profitability.

My personal takeaways from this experience that I applied throughout my career and that we will expand upon in this chapter are to not take assumptions and expectations at face value, even if they are based upon historical experience. Assumptions and expectations should be validated to make sure they in fact yield the best results available to meet executive objectives.

Additionally, just because there is initial validation of the assumptions and expectations being used when a strategy is selected, it is critical to create an integrated relationship between operations and finance that continuously validates the assumptions and expectations based on the feedback of the actual conditions that exist at any point in time.

Cash

I love to ask executives to give me one word that describes the most critical requirement for the survival and growth of an organization.

I add that it is equally critical for growth, stability, and survival and is a major cause for the failure of an organization.

While I get great answers like people, service, sales, and acceptance—the answer is cash.

The lyrics of the song "Money," from the musical *Cabaret*—"money makes the world go around"—could not be more accurate than in the world of organizational survival.[9]

This is why the C-suite intuitively wants to understand the cost and budget associated with a strategic initiative.

Unfortunately, while important, the determination and analysis of such a budget is only one piece of the puzzle. Surprisingly, even continuous close monitoring of the actual cost versus the budget for an initiative does not complete the puzzle.

Maybe because of my combined background in finance, accounting, and operations, I finally realized what the missing piece of the puzzle was.

It is a determination and continuous focus on the real underlying executive objectives behind any given strategic initiative.

In general terms, the use of cash for a strategic initiative comes down to just one of three executive objectives: (a) use some cash now (the strategic initiative budget) to generate more cash over time in the future (growth), (b) use some cash now (the strategic initiative budget) to use less cash over time in the future (improved operational efficiency), or (c) some combination of the two.

The missing piece of the puzzle is the determination, monitoring, and control of these objectives from a cash management perspective within an ever-changing, dynamic environment.

Fortunately, it is not missing from the Dynamic Execution framework described in this book.

Instead, for any given objective and associated strategic initiative, Dynamic Execution incorporates the establishment, documentation, and analysis of the critical factors and assumptions associated with these objectives; creates an integration of daily operational activities with finance for continuous and timely analysis; and continuously monitors and analyzes the actual conditions that are dynamically taking place versus the expected critical factors and assumptions.

Dynamic Execution provides ongoing and *immediate* analytical financial feedback to operations and the rest of the organization, including executives. This feedback is then used for evaluation of status, analysis, and control. If necessary, adjustments can be made to the assumptions, structure of the strategic initiative, and/or expectations associated with the objective.

This represents an analytical cash management capability *embedded* into a closed-loop continuous system, a system that uses feedback loops to provide organization-wide bidirectional communication.

Communications of expectations, critical factors, and assumptions down into the organization and communication of input into expectations and assumptions, along with information generated from ongoing monitoring and analysis, upwards into the organization.

Finance: A Special Role In Dynamic Execution

Since the control and management of cash plays such an essential role within an organization, having an analytical review from a financial/cash perspective embedded within the Dynamic Execution methodology becomes a powerful tool—a tool that does not replace, but extends well beyond, simply project budgeting.

The monitoring of actual conditions against critical factors and assumptions by operations can and will reveal unexpected disconnects that need to be assessed.

The assessment needs to go beyond just operational considerations and include an analysis from a financial/cash management perspective. This financial analysis can range from very simple to highly complex modeling and analysis. However, it should be recognized that in most cases, this does not have to be complex but can be a straightforward and a relatively simple set of activities.

First, when an objective is developed, the expectations associated with the objective will already have been established. However, it is very important that expectations are not the only thing documented. All of the critical factors and major assumptions associated with those expectations also need to be clearly documented.

This information then provides a basis for financial modeling and analytical validation that the assumptions and critical factors will, in fact, yield the expected results.

In essence, the assumptions become the variables in the modeling/analysis, while the critical factors represent requirements associated with the strategy/process selected to obtain the desired objective.

For example, let's say the objective is to increase this year's margins via an increase in sales obtained through an improvement in the launch date of a new release of one of your software application offerings.

Based upon feedback received from within the organization, your expectation is that a six-month advancement of the launch date will result in a $250,000 improvement in sales.

The strategy to advance the launch date is to reassign staffing to specifically focus on the debugging of the software update.

The reassigned staff represents a critical factor, and a major assumption is that the accelerated focus on debugging will yield a six-month reduction to the launch date.

Finance then analyzes the expectations, critical factors, and assumptions, which indicate that if the cost of the reassigned resource is $50,000 (another assumption), a $250,000 increase in sales after other normal cost of sales expenses will yield an increase in the margin of $125,000 (another expectation).

From a financial analysis perspective, the critical factor of the reassignment of staff represents a requirement of the selected process.

The assumptions of the six-month improvement in the launch date and the $50,000 cost of reassignment are variables in the financial analysis.

In other words, any sort of analysis of this selected strategic initiative must include the cost of reassigned resources.

Any variation in either the actual length of the improvement in the launch date or the actual cost of the reassigned resources will directly affect the expectation, that is, the amount of additional margin generated from the initiative.

Feedback on expectations, critical factors, and assumptions are now communicated to the organization so that they are continuously monitored against actual conditions.

Feedback on any issues or variations (disconnects) in these conditions would immediately be communicated to finance. Finance then analyzes the effects on expectations, which are then communicated back to the organization.

The organization and executives now have the most current information possible to immediately determine if any reconsiderations or adjustments are needed.

More importantly, this new information includes an assessment of the financial impact to assist in the decision-making process. Any immediately required actions represent feedback to be communicated to the organization.

This structure epitomizes a continuously functioning integrated closed-loop system.

Integration Of Operations

Once again, I use the term operations of an organization in a very broad context. While functional areas of responsibility from one organization to another can vary significantly, the use of the term operations comprises all functional areas unique to any given organization.

These could include everything from R&D/engineering/product development to marketing/sales, to production/distribution/service/customer support, to IT/HR/finance/accounting, and so on.

In other words, the use of the term operations includes any functional area involved in the day-to-day activities associated with the creation, production, distribution, and support of products or services to the marketplace/users.

As previously indicated, this broad-based framework is used because, from a strategic development and execution perspective, all current and future systems and procedures used anywhere within an organization originate from the execution of strategic initiatives.

In addition, strategic initiative executions almost always require cross-functional involvement and feedback. They also often affect systems and procedures in a multifunctional context.

Therefore, the executive goal of blending strategic initiatives with a day-to-day operations structure is best accomplished when it is viewed from the perspective of a fully integrated cross-functional organization.

Unfortunately, the ability to attain this sort of integrated cross-functional structure can be easier said than done.

Fortunately, over my career, I have had firsthand experience in many functional areas acquired across different types of organizations.

My experience is extremely diversified, covering forty technology, manufacturing, distribution, and service sectors that range from leading-edge technology products and services to high-growth, high-tech, green products and services to traditional automotive and mainstream manufacturing, distribution, and service operations.

This diversified firsthand experience allowed me to better understand the challenges associated with achieving an integrated and amalgamated cross-functional structure. It also allowed me to better understand and directly relate to the perspective of the positive and negative communications I was receiving from individuals within various functional areas.

However, as an executive, I also recognized that the overall performance of an organization could not be maximized unless all of these functional areas were executed in an integrated context toward a common, well-defined set of objectives.

Finally, I recognize that the integration of functional areas within an organization is, in reality, an extremely difficult C-suite challenge.

For example, as an executive, I have walked into a cross-functional meeting knowing several things. Product development was under a great deal of pressure to finalize a product or service offering for the market that sales were already promoting in the marketplace. Sales were under pressure to make sure adequate demand existed for these offerings that were not yet fully available, and that might still be subject to changes in functionality. Production was under pressure to efficiently and effectively coordinate the phasing in of the new and the phasing out of the existing offering. Customer support was under pressure to develop a support program that would be immediately available when the distribution began for the new offering that had not yet been fully defined or completed. Finance was under pressure to try to provide controls and feedback on the costs of development, release, and ultimate margins associated with the new offering.

Typical comments during the meeting included different concerns from different departments.

Product development: "How can you be trying to sell an offering that is not even completed?"

Sales: "Why can't you even tell us when the functionality will be fully developed and the offering will be available for distribution?"

Production: "We echo the sales concern about the lack of a completion date and ask sales why they cannot provide good projections of the demand for the phasing out of the existing offering and initial demand for the new offering."

Customer support: "Given that support programs vary by the type of customer, we need to know what specific customers will be involved in the initial distribution and be trained on the differences between the existing and new offerings."

Finance: "Is there a variation from the original budget, and will the final cost structure of the new offering still support the required margin based on the go-to-market selling price?"

As an executive, try to tell everyone to perform in an integrated context when each area has its own set of pressures that (a) are out of their direct control and interdependent upon other areas within the organization, (b) are very time-sensitive, but the actual timing of a launch event is completely unknown, (c) represent extensive time commitments, which are in addition to existing day-to-day operational activities, and (d) induce frustration around required activities because backs are up against the wall and require last-minute attention.

Unfortunately, these dynamics all take place within a reality that the ongoing existence of the organization is best served through an integrated amalgamation of activities across functional areas.

And, while failure within any one of those areas represents a risk to the organization, ongoing organizational success is dependent on an integrated execution of the activities within all pertinent areas.

So, how do executives create such an integrated organization?

Addressing this challenge and creating an integrated organization lies in the following activities. There must be a strong belief, desire, and confidence within the C-suite that an integrated organization is possible and, if successfully executed, represents a major competitive advantage. The rest of the organization will quickly detect a lack of confidence or lack of desire to have a truly integrated organizational structure. Therefore, all executives must continually reinforce and communicate their focus on the requirement for integration across all functional areas.

The C-suite must make it clear and insist that while every functional area needs to perform as effectively and efficiently as possible, they must all operate as an integrated component of the entire organization.

This represents a structure where all functional areas operate in a cohesive, unified context. It is not the same as teamwork, where people are expected to work together toward a common objective. *Instead, think of it in the context of the human body, where each function operates as a separate system but is interconnected, integrated, and, most importantly, interdependent in such a way that they must act as one to perform properly and survive. Integration requires that all functional areas are unified and focused on a common set of goals and objectives.*

Don't deny or discount the dynamics and frustrations discussed above that are occurring within the functional areas regarding strategic execution and daily operational activities. They are a reality that often exists and, therefore, must be addressed.

Instead, create an understanding and buy-in within the organization about the true strategic and organizational dynamics interrelationship. Point out that all of the systems and procedures being used in day-to-day operations (daily activity) are the result of historically executed strategic initiatives. It will be through newly executed strategic initiatives that future systems, methods, and procedures used in day-to-day operations will be created and modified.

Therefore, instead of implementation plans that are created and driven down into a functional area, strategic initiative activities must be blended with day-to-day operational activities within and across every functional area. This blending recognizes that to support the ongoing objective for continuous improvements in performance and the organization's long-term survival, daily activities and responsibilities within every functional area need to include a focus on strategic and operational requirements.

Describe how this blending will include the introduction of feedback loops to help create an integrated system for communication, broad-based input, and unification among all of the functional areas. *Indicate how these feedback loops are like the nervous system in the human body, with input, feedback, and information constantly flowing bidirectionally throughout the entire organization. Therefore, like the human body, each functional area can operate separately but in a unified, integrated context.*

Explain how, in the future, the expectations, critical factors, and assumptions associated with strategic initiatives will be analyzed, documented, and monitored in order to enhance the ability to obtain a successful execution.

This approach will focus the blending of the strategic activities within a functional area on specific efforts and areas to concentrate on that are essential to the successful execution of a strategic initiative. It will leverage off of feedback loops for the solicitation of functional-area input into the analysis of critical factors and assumptions and the communication back into the functional areas of strategic objectives and critical information.

The approach will strengthen organizational integration and unification through a continuous bidirectional flow across all functional areas of the comprehensive data required to obtain the desired objective.

Finally, executives need to embrace a more enhanced and comprehensive human-resource management system that is better suited to support and reinforce an integrated organizational structure.

The objective is to expand an organization's evaluation criteria beyond just skill set and performance. They need to include consideration of the following critical areas: (a) contribution to strategic initiative execution and productivity improvements, (b) contribution to innovation, (c) level of cross-training, (d) capability to support organizational growth, and (e) areas of interest and willingness to participate.

Incorporating these expanded criteria reinforces the significance of acceptance and participation in an integrated and blended strategic execution/operations structure throughout the organization.

This is an organization-wide HR management system. Therefore, it can be an exceptionally effective executive tool for communicating directly to the management of a functional area the significance and expectations of having an integrated and unified organization structure that includes the functional area under their control.

In summary, while many of the Dynamic Execution and executive concepts and tools presented in this book can be utilized without having the fully integrated cross-functional organization structure outlined here, the ability to maximize your success is greatly enhanced when such a structure is in place.

The key to such an integrated structure lies first in dedicated and continuous communication by executives to the organization that it is a priority. It is then preferably reinforced through the incorporation of pertinent considerations within the HR evaluation and management system.

It is also important to recognize that the blending of strategic initiative and daily operational activities is not just some open-ended, free-form mode of doing business.

It is a highly organized, disciplined system requiring (a) participation and input in the analysis of conditions, critical factors, and assumptions, (b) when applicable, execution of specific assigned tasks associated with a strategic initiative, and (c) the monitoring and communication of actual conditions versus the critical factors and assumptions related to strategic initiatives.

This is a process that is supported through a configuration of top-to-bottom feedback loops.

The Who

A very relevant question that is often asked is, "Who exactly is going to do many of these coordination efforts?"

Consistent with my earlier responses to similar discussions on responsibilities, depending on the size of the organization, it is the middle management (directors/senior managers) and junior/VPs level executives. If you revisit figures 5.3 and 5.4 together with figure 5.5, you see that it is middle management, such as directors/senior managers and junior/VP level executives, that are at the center of the development and oversight of the execution of strategies along with the blending of the strategic and operational activities for the accomplishment of the objectives.

These positions are where you see the swing from a primarily operational focus, such as with operations managers and execution staff, to the primarily strategic focus of senior management. *So, you can think of middle management as the spinal cord of an organization with significant roles in both operations and strategy. Therefore, this group is in the best position to take responsibility for the necessary coordination activities.*

As a side note, I often find that the significance of the roles middle management plays is poorly understood or defined and, therefore, improperly leveraged. This can lead to major missed opportunities for executives in their ability to reach their objectives.

One Last Analogy: I Want To Exit This Building

As mentioned above, an integrated, unified, blended organization can be viewed as analogous to the human body.

Like an organization, the human anatomy has multiple independent but integrated systems working together to create a functioning entity with a purpose.

The body as a whole can be equated to the top-to-bottom, all-inclusive operations of an organization. Life in both entities is maintained by the day-to-day activities and output from operations of the functioning components.

Objectives in both are established and strategic initiatives are blended with operations to be executed to accomplish the desired results. The nervous system acts just like the bidirectional feedback loops to communicate objectives and strategic initiatives outwards from the brain while communicating inwards to the brain the existing internal and external conditions that are actually present.

Illustration: Assume an individual is located somewhere inside of a building.

They determine that they want to leave and go outside (the objective) by walking to and out a door (walking to the door, opening the door, and walking out is the strategic initiative, and the door is a critical factor).

They walk up to a door only to find it locked and with no key (inaccurate/missed assumption regarding a critical factor).

The feedback of the locked door is instantaneously communicated back up to the brain, and an outward communication is issued to find and try another door (modified strategic initiative).

The blending of strategic execution with operations allows the focus to shift slightly toward execution of the new strategic initiative so the legs move a little faster and the heart pumps a little quicker (a dynamic adjustment in the various functional area's activities to support the new strategic execution).

The next door is located and opened, and the individual exits the building (strategic initiative is executed, and the desired objective is obtained).

The body relaxes back to a normal state of operations while the next set of objectives are determined (operations communicate to the brain the current conditions that exist for consideration and analysis).

This example highlights that the body is *not* a strict choice between strategic execution *or* day-to-day operational activities.

The body does not die because there has been a shift in focus toward strategic execution. Nor is there a desire for the body to come to an uncoordinated standstill because the focus is shifted toward the operational activities associated with each functional system.

Therefore, the blending of strategic execution and operational activities provides an immediate and continuous ability to adjust the balance between strategic and operational activities based on the actual conditions and objectives that exist at any point in time.

PART V

Dynamic Execution

Core Activities

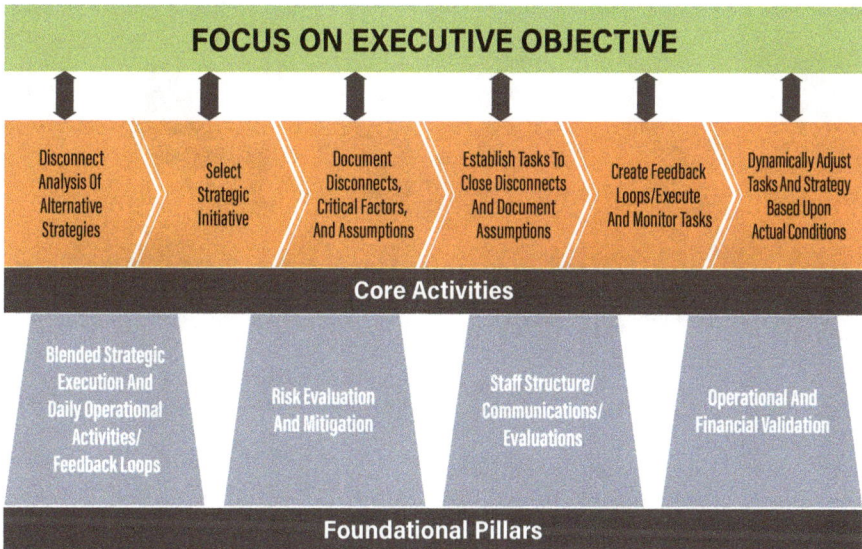

FOCUS ON EXECUTIVE OBJECTIVE					

| Disconnect Analysis Of Alternative Strategies | Select Strategic Initiative | Document Disconnects, Critical Factors, And Assumptions | Establish Tasks To Close Disconnects And Document Assumptions | Create Feedback Loops/Execute And Monitor Tasks | Dynamically Adjust Tasks And Strategy Based Upon Actual Conditions |

Core Activities

Blended Strategic Execution And Daily Operational Activities/ Feedback Loops	Risk Evaluation And Mitigation	Staff Structure/ Communications/ Evaluations	Operational And Financial Validation

Foundational Pillars

Chapters 13, 14, and 15 connect the process all together by detailing innovative concepts, tools, and techniques for the accomplishment of Dynamic Execution core activities.

13

Dynamic Execution Core Activities
Thirty-Thousand-Foot Executive Overview

Given current and historical failure rates, I know for many, it is hard to believe, even incomprehensible, that there are innovative concepts, tools, and methodologies that can drastically improve your strategic execution success rate. It is even harder to imagine that executives can obtain these sorts of results in a fraction of the time compared to what is usually encountered. Just imagine the ability to:

- Implement and launch an entirely new, top-to-bottom, enterprise-wide system in a large organization in less than four months—and execute it without disrupting on-time delivery, customer satisfaction, or financial reporting.
- Integrate major acquisitions in four to six months.
- Obtain a tenfold increase in productivity in a matter of months.
- Put together and execute a major financial recapitalization in less than six months.
- Maintain and even improve profitability during periods of recession, inflation, and employment challenges.
- Move thousands of square feet of manufacturing facilities over a weekend without disruption to on-time delivery.
- Turn inventory in a complex manufacturing operation once a week (yes, fifty-two times a year).

- Have a 35 percent margin in an industry that only averages 11 percent.
- Provide monthly consolidated financial statements in a major international organization, including taking a worldwide physical inventory, in just three days.

This is just a sample of the results obtained through the use of Dynamic Execution and the other concepts, tools, and methodologies discussed in this book.

Up to this point, I have provided a lot of details and actionable concepts, tools, and solutions to help executives increase the success rate for the execution of their vital objectives.

I have established and explained the four pillars of a Dynamic Execution foundation:

- A blended strategic execution and operations organization structure with feedback loops
- Enhanced risk-management capabilities built from a scientific and expanded understanding of the dynamics of risk
- New innovative concepts and methodologies for human-resource management
- Capabilities to obtain the validation of selected management objectives and execution strategies through operational and financial integration

It is now time to complete the picture of how this all comes together under the umbrella of Dynamic Execution by exploring the core activities presented in figure 13.1.

Figure 13.1

Dynamic Execution Core Activities

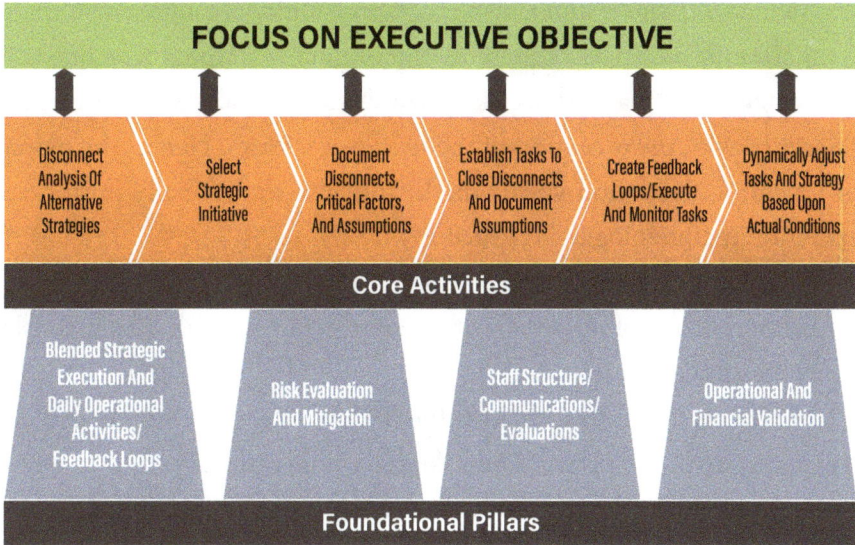

FOCUS ON EXECUTIVE OBJECTIVE

| Disconnect Analysis Of Alternative Strategies | Select Strategic Initiative | Document Disconnects, Critical Factors, And Assumptions | Establish Tasks To Close Disconnects And Document Assumptions | Create Feedback Loops/Execute And Monitor Tasks | Dynamically Adjust Tasks And Strategy Based Upon Actual Conditions |

Core Activities

| Blended Strategic Execution And Daily Operational Activities/ Feedback Loops | Risk Evaluation And Mitigation | Staff Structure/ Communications/ Evaluations | Operational And Financial Validation |

Foundational Pillars

Starting Considerations From What We Have Learned So Far

Most importantly, from an executive perspective, success should be strictly focused on obtaining the important objectives they want to attain as quickly as possible.

I have found this perspective gets lost in the shuffle once a specific execution strategy and associated implementation methodology/plan have been selected. As I have mentioned, it amazes me how often the focus of obtaining a critical objective is hijacked once a specific strategy and implementation plan to accomplish an objective has been selected. Instead, the focus is no longer on making sure the objective is obtained; it shifts to trying to prove that the strategy and implementation plan selected were an accurate and best choice.

Strategic initiative executions take place in a world of constantly changing conditions. New conditions are not only difficult to predict accurately but can be uncontrollable and require decisions to be made based on a significant set of assumptions.

Therefore, there is inherently a high probability of failure when there is an attempt to strictly adhere to the originally selected strategy and implementation plan. This risk increases substantially as the timeline associated with the execution of the strategy increases. Hence, the power of Dynamic Execution versus the historically traditionally promoted execution methodologies is created.

All processes, procedures, and systems currently at play in the day-to-day operations of an organization are the direct result of previously executed strategic initiatives.

Therefore, any future changes (be it large or small) to these day-to-day operational systems will only take place under the execution of a new strategic initiative. Consequently, day-to-day activities should be viewed as an ongoing combination of both the operational activities of supplying goods and services and the strategic execution activities associated with changes to operational processes, procedures, and systems. Once again, there is enormous power in dynamic integration and the blending of operational and strategic execution activities.

A Thirty-Thousand-Foot Executive Guide For Dynamic Execution Core Activities

The overall goal of Dynamic Execution is to significantly increase the probability of successfully executing strategic initiatives that will effectively yield the established executive/organizational objectives.

Key steps embedded in the core activities:

1. Determine actual current conditions and critical strategy requirements based on the established organizational objective.
2. Determine organizational disconnects between actual conditions and critical requirements, including any functionality trade-offs and/or "when not if" considerations.

3. Comprehensively and clearly document disconnects and critical factors, along with any assumptions used in the selection of the strategy and/or within the disconnect analysis.

4. Analyze, document, and continuously monitor potential risk factors. If you have a controllable risk factor, then that risk factor should be eliminated, provided the significance of the risk factor justifies the time, effort, and cost of elimination. If the risk factor is uncontrollable, then, when possible, that risk factor should be mitigated, provided the significance of the risk factor justifies the time, effort, and cost of mitigation.

5. Perform initial financial modeling and analytical validation that the critical factors and assumptions of the selected strategy will, in fact, yield the expected results.

6. For the selected strategic initiative, define and document the tasks required to close each disconnect and the assumptions used, such as timing and critical-resource requirement considerations.

7. For each defined task or, when appropriate, group of tasks, perform a resource-to-disconnect analysis to determine the time, effort, and capability requirements associated with the completion of each task.

8. For the selected strategy and each task, document the specific conditions, critical requirements, and assumptions to be used as monitoring and feedback criteria. Utilize these criteria to establish monitoring integration points within the operational feedback loop structure.

9. Dynamically schedule and execute the tasks focusing on such considerations as:

   a. The time, effort, and capability requirements established through the resource-to-disconnect analysis.

   b. Advanced critical assumption testing opportunities. These represent opportunities to test in advance, or early on in the execution, critical assumptions regarding such things as expected effectiveness or benefits from the execution of the selected strategy. For example, will a given process work as expected, or is a specific assumption correct, and will it yield the expected results? The advanced or early testing or execution of these tasks and associated processes can help avoid unexpected issues and greatly accelerate the execution timeline.

c. A determination of nonsequential versus sequential scheduling opportunities. Ask which tasks are interdependent (either sequentially or for some other reason) with the execution of other tasks versus which tasks can be executed independent of the sequential execution of other tasks. This information can be used to effectively set priorities and perform simultaneous execution activities, once again accelerating the execution timeline.

d. "When not if" considerations.

e. Feedback from the continuous monitoring of actual conditions, critical criteria, and risks.

10. Perform continuous monitoring, analysis, and feedback of actual conditions to strategy, disconnect, assumption criteria, and risk.

a. Based on feedback of actual conditions, perform updated financial and cash management modeling, analysis, and revalidation.

b. Modify tasks and/or selected strategies based upon the feedback of deviations between actual conditions and the critical required conditions and assumptions.

c. Continue this process until objective expectations and "when not if" criteria are successfully achieved.

Note: Additional detailed information and guidance will be explored in chapters 14 and 15.

Six Major Dynamic Execution Differentiators

One: **A Focus On The Tasks Required To Close Specifically Defined Disconnects**

One of the biggest differentiators between the Dynamic Execution methodology and historically used strategic execution and implementation methodologies is a focus on the tasks required to close specifically defined disconnects.

As discussed earlier, under traditional approaches, solution sets/ strategies are typically selected based on having the functionality needed to provide the capabilities necessary to accomplish the organizational objective. An example could be the functionality found in a certain vendor's software system, a piece of equipment, operational configuration, or staffing structure. Once it is determined that the selected solution set has the required functionality, the focus becomes the implementation of that specific functionality and the associated selected solution.

This focus is often reinforced by the hype that the selected solution set is proven in the marketplace, and therefore, if you do not obtain the functionality, you have done something wrong.

Unfortunately, these traditional approaches are missing a number of realities. The conditions in every organization are different. Therefore, the disconnects and functionality trade-offs will be different, leading to different levels of effort, potential issues, and appropriateness for the accomplishment of the objective.

This is the real reason, in most cases, proven functionality and implementation methodologies fail. It is not that the organization did anything wrong; it is because there is not a clear recognition of the actual disconnects that exist, leading to unexpected challenges and the need for extended execution timelines.

Dynamic Execution focuses up front on the actual disconnects, functionality trade-offs, assumptions, and tasks required to make a specific strategy work. Therefore, the organization obtains a superior indication of not just the effort and potential issues but of the overall fit and risks associated with the strategy/solution.

Another missing reality of traditional methodologies is that the selected strategy and functionality are based upon the conditions that exist at the specific point in time the selection is made. Therefore, there is an unrealistic reliance on the ability to accurately predict future conditions and that the assumptions used when selecting the strategy and functionality are correct. In turn, this leads to an unwillingness to make any necessary adjustments to the selected strategy and/or implementation plan.

Dynamic Execution clearly defines and continuously monitors the actual conditions that exist versus the critical requirements and assumptions associated with the selected strategy and tasks. It recognizes the inherent dynamics of perpetually changing conditions and dictates that the tasks, and possibly even the selected strategy itself, might need to be modified in order to obtain what is really important: the accomplishment of the objective.

Finally, the recognition of these inherent dynamics leads to the incorporation of a major focus on reducing the execution timeline in order to minimize the exposure to continuously changing conditions.

Two: A Continuous Blending Of Strategic Execution Activities With Day-To-Day Operational Activities

A second major differentiator is the recognition that the most effective and efficient way to obtain the successful execution of strategic initiatives is through a continuous blending of strategic execution activities with day-to-day operational activities.

Traditional approaches focus on strategic initiatives as projects to be implemented. This leads to internal conflict, confusion, unnecessary disruption to day-to-day operational activities, and increases the timeline associated with the execution.

Dynamic Execution recognizes that in order to have changes to existing operations, there must be the execution of a strategic initiative. It realizes that an organization is operating in an environment that has constantly changing conditions. Therefore, the strategic executions required to adjust the daily operational systems to address these new conditions must also be (and, in fact, are) a continuous set of activities.

It is only logical that these dynamics need to be recognized and an organization structure created with an ongoing continuous daily blending of required strategic execution activities and required operational activities.

There are many advantages to this structure.

First, individuals, departments, and the organization have the ability to adjust the daily activities they focus on based on the existing strategic and operational workload.

It is no different than the activities associated with simultaneously supplying multiple types of products or services. Demand can fluctuate daily and, therefore, the focus/activity required to support these operational activities also fluctuates. Individuals, departments, and the organization recognize this, and the flexibility to schedule and adjust their activities to the actual priorities and conditions that exist becomes assumed as a normal part of executing daily operational activities.

However, now these workloads include activities associated with strategic execution, which, like customer demand, can fluctuate. Therefore, the blending of strategic and operational activities provides the same flexibility to dynamically schedule and adapt to changing priorities and conditions.

Another advantage of this blending is that it drives responsibilities, control, and involvement down to the lowest level possible.

Unlike traditional approaches, it is not a workload or expectation jammed into the daily routines of staff by third parties or individuals assigned the difficult task of making a certain project successful.

Instead, the continuous blending of necessary strategic execution activities with daily operational activities is an ongoing responsibility over which individuals and departments have at least some levels of control and involvement in.

In other words, this responsibility for involvement in strategic execution represents actual staff empowerment.

It helps staff recognize and accept the significance of both operational and strategic activities, enhancing their willingness to be involved.

There is also the advantage that a continuous blending of strategic and operational activities creates a structure that can significantly reduce execution timelines.

First, it builds a certain amount of ongoing available capacity into the system. Next, it creates an ability to simultaneously support multiple strategic initiative executions and shift priorities and resource utilization in a dynamic context.

However, it does not do this in an unstructured framework.

To the contrary, what makes Dynamic Execution work is a very structured approach that starts, and constantly continues, with a focus on obtaining a given objective.

It then clearly focuses on the disconnects that exist within the organization to accomplish that objective along with a willingness to adjust if required by the actual future conditions that exists.

It is the clear and comprehensive understanding and documentation of expectations, disconnects, assumptions, and risks that provide the basis for an organization-wide communication and execution to accomplish the objective.

It is completed with the use of organization-wide feedback loops. These not only provide an excellent structure for bidirectional communication of required inputs and continuous monitoring but also support staff involvement and empowerment.

Finally, there is a major advantage in that—when continuous improvement is applied to strategic execution in a blended strategic/operations organization structure—the benefits derived from the successful accomplishment of objectives will yield the creation and perpetuation of available staff resources.

In other words, over time, this structure represents a system that self-generates the ability to provide the staffing resources necessary to support the continuous execution of future objectives.

Executives commit a portion of existing staff resources through the blending of strategic execution responsibilities with daily operational responsibilities. These committed resources execute objectives that generate additional staffing capacity.

For example, if an objective generates additional revenues, the profitability from those added revenues provides the ability to support additional staffing. If an objective produces improved operational efficiencies, those efficiencies yield additional available capacity from existing staff. This new additional capacity can then support the execution of the next set of executive objectives, ultimately making this a self-generating, self-supporting, self-feeding perpetual system.

Three: Use Of Feedback Loops And The Monitoring Of Actual-To-Expected Conditions

The use of feedback loops and the monitoring of actual-to-expected conditions is another major differentiator.

These structured feedback loops provide a communication vehicle for input on existing conditions and participation in strategy development, selection, and analysis. They also provide for the easy organization-wide communication of details associated with the *why, when, who,* and *how* of a strategic initiative.

Finally, feedback loops support the bidirectional communication for the monitoring, analysis, financial validation, and adjustments required during the execution of the initiative.

Traditional approaches also incorporate and rely on various sorts of communication methodologies. Unfortunately, once again, these approaches and structures tend to be project oriented and vary from project to project in approach, content, and focus.

On the other hand, the feedback loop structure is intended to be incorporated into the fabric of the organization.

This structure is agnostic and is not focused on a one-off strategic initiative but will support the simultaneous development and execution of multiple strategic initiatives in a consistent, continuous, and repeatable framework.

Four: Standardized Methods For The Financial Determination And Control Of A Strategic Initiative's Performance And Cost

In the traditional world, there is variation in the methods used for the financial determination and control of a strategic initiative's performance and cost.

In addition, solution and mythology selections can often be negatively influenced by the inherent marketplace dynamics associated with the financial rewards that experts, service providers, and consultants derive from the promotion and execution of their specific services and methodologies.

While Dynamic Execution does not exclude some of the traditional tools, such as budgets, it does differentiate itself in several significant ways.

One of these is performance. Dynamic Execution incorporates the use of financial modeling for the validation that the critical factors and assumptions associated with a strategic initiative will in fact yield an objective's expectations. This analysis and validation are performed both up front and whenever necessary based upon the ongoing monitoring and feedback of actual conditions.

Another differentiation is cost. Dynamic Execution enhances the ability to develop a more comprehensive review and analysis of cost drivers. It drills down on specific cost drivers that are represented by an analysis of specific disconnects, functionality trade-offs, assumptions, and potential risks.

In addition, it addresses the shortfalls associated with energy/effort/capability hump disconnects found in traditional methodologies with a much more powerful resource-to-disconnect analysis. This provides a set of much richer and detailed data for the determination of both actual and potential costs.

Five: Dynamic Execution Is Applicable And Scalable To Any Size Organization, Initiative, Or Objective

The Dynamic Execution concepts, tools, techniques, and approaches discussed in this book are applicable and scalable to any size organization, initiative, or objective.

It must be recognized that disconnects between required critical factors and actual conditions, along with perpetually changing conditions, apply to any type of strategic change: big or small, departmental or organizational.

Plus, providing strategic execution capacity through a blended strategic/operations structure, advanced testing, and assumption monitoring/feedback represent powerful tools for any size organization or for any critical strategic execution that needs to be successful.

Six: Dynamic Execution Represents A Straightforward But Comprehensive Closed-Loop Structure That Is Easy To Understand And Use

In the end, Dynamic Execution differentiates itself through a straightforward but comprehensive closed-loop structure that is easy to understand and use.

It clearly spells out and explains how to understand, monitor, control, and compensate for all of the dynamics/complexity that intrinsically exist in order to accomplish successful organizational objectives.

Dynamic Execution goes on to challenge and can destroy the long timelines that are so often inappropriately established for strategic execution.

Finally, Dynamic Execution provides executives an effective and efficient capability to plug into and monitor the development, selection, and execution of the strategic initiatives required to obtain the organizational objectives they so desperately desire.

14

Deep Dive Into Dynamic Execution Core Activities
Steps One To Four

Illustration: During my career, I frequently had the executive responsibility of overseeing the major merger of a newly acquired organization. In most cases, this included a complete integration of both financial and operational systems.

The established objectives from our executives were to (a) integrate operations between the acquired organization and existing operations to obtain improved efficiencies and profitability, (b) execute revenue improvement and cost reduction opportunities within the acquired organization, and (c) integrate the acquired organization's financial systems to meet the requirements of existing corporate accounting and reporting systems.

Given the size and complexity of these mergers, it was common for traditional integration consultants, accounting firms, and other mergers-and-acquisitions experts to predict a time frame of at least a year or more in addition to a significant commitment of cost and resources.

However, my experience indicated that any merger/integration that took more than six months would, in fact, yield terrible results.

In addition, the cost and resource commitments were overstated and unnecessary.

Six months, at most, was the window of opportunity before the needed flexibility, pliability, and cooperation of the staff at the acquired organization would cease to be available to obtain a successful integration. Beyond six months, it became more and more difficult and costly to implement the changes required to accomplish all of the objectives.

Therefore, my target was always four to six months at most. It was not uncommon for the local management of the acquired organization to expect me to be involved for an extended period, to which I would reply, "If I am involved for more than six months, I will have failed."

My success in accomplishing these objectives in such a short period can be traced to the utilization of the core Dynamic Execution activities I am about to explain in more detail.

At the highest level, the activities associated with these efforts can be summarized as follows.

- Leverage the existing knowledge base of the conditions, assumptions, critical factors, and expectations (objectives) available from the decision-making process utilized when opting to acquire the organization.

- Immediately determine the actual conditions at the acquired organization to ascertain the critical disconnects that exist. Simultaneously, focus on establishing and executing the tasks required to address them.

- Immediately upon the closing of the acquisition, begin to establish a staffing infrastructure (blended operations and strategic execution) that would execute the ongoing strategic executions and tasks required to obtain both current and future desired executive objectives.

- Establish the monitoring criteria, monitoring points, and feedback loops necessary for an efficient capability for ongoing corporate executive oversight and management of strategic executions and objective management.

Important: What Needs To Be Understood For This All To Make Sense

In general, I find that in a broad context, executives do not have issues with understanding the discussions and innovative concepts I have presented thus far in this book.

It is not difficult to follow the discussions surrounding the four foundational pillars of Dynamic Execution: (a) blended strategic execution and daily operational activities with feedback loops, (b) risk evaluation and mitigation, (c) staff structure/communications/evaluations, and (d) operational and financial validation and integration.

Even the thirty-thousand-foot overview of the Dynamic Execution core activities presented in chapter 13 tends to avoid confusion.

What I do find is that, as I delve into the following deeper operational aspects of the Dynamic Execution core activities, executives really begin to see just how big a paradigm shift Dynamic Execution is compared to traditional organizational structures, staff integration, risk management, and strategic execution.

It is like telling someone raised on using maps to navigate from one location to the next that there is a new way to do it: GPS. Or, telling someone who has been forced for years to get their groceries from the local supermarket that they can now acquire them via their phone and have them delivered.

The reaction is, "Wait a second, how does this really work?" "What do I need to do to make this happen?"

So, before we take a more comprehensive look at the actual execution of core activities, I want to review some central concepts of Dynamic Execution that are often initially missed but are fundamental to your understanding of how and why this works.

- *Dynamic Execution represents a structure for continuous improvement that is integrated into the fabric of the organization.* It provides continuous improvement derived from the constant execution of strategic initiatives that produce the accomplishment of successful objectives.

- *The focus is not on the execution of projects.* Strategic execution leading to improvement through accomplished objectives is instead an ongoing integrated responsibility of everyone in the organization.
- *Everyone has some level of defined responsibility to assist in the execution of strategies that promote the advancement of the organization.* This responsibility is built into the composition of everyone's responsibilities.

Why is this important to understand?

Traditionally, staff responsibility and involvement in an execution/change initiative is piecemeal.

There is usually an individual or core group (like a department) that assumes (or is forced to assume) primary responsibility for the execution.

It is then up to them, either through the use of external or internal resources, to determine and, when necessary, sell a selected solution, establish a plan that is often cross-functional, and then try to solicit and coordinate the participation necessary to make the project successful.

As discussed earlier, this is all done with little ability to consider or adjust for everyone's existing workloads and time commitments.

Even with the use of cross-functional and hopefully cooperative coordination meetings and dedicated project managers, this process is extremely inefficient, clumsy, time-consuming, often political, and prone to failure.

For example, I cannot tell you how many times I have heard someone say, "Well, that's your project; I have my own work and projects to get done."

With this as an often-found frame of reference, I know when we start looking at the detailed steps involved in the execution of core activities, there will be executives who will be asking, "How is this going to work?" or "Where are these staffing resources coming from?"

All good questions.

Now for the answers.

First, I would suggest that a quick review of the figures and content in chapter 5 will be helpful. Figure 5.6 indicates how the percentage of staff time committed to the development and strategic execution of objectives increases significantly as you move up the organization structure. By the time you reach the senior manager and director levels in an organization, objective development and strategic execution can, and in most cases should, represent 40 percent or more of the staff's responsibilities.

Therefore, progression up the organizational hierarchy represents an increasingly core group focused on objective development and strategic execution. This is further reinforced in figures 5.3 and 5.4, which outline the specific responsibilities by position. This then represents a continuous focus on organizational improvements through the successful accomplishment of objectives (objective management).

The focus is always on objective management. It must be recognized that these assigned responsibilities are organization-wide and not limited to strictly the activities of a given individual, department, or functional area. This makes strategic responsibilities inherently cross-functional and cross-organizational. Everyone is working toward and, when necessary, is responsible for the accomplishment of all established organizational objectives.

Strategic executions are for the accomplishment of established objectives that are ultimately beneficial to the entire organization. Therefore, even strategic execution activities approved through the core activities process that are primarily focused on a specific area within the organization should be viewed as a part of everyone's responsibility.

For example, assume the C-suite objective is to improve operating margins by 10 percent. Through the Dynamic Execution core activities process, it is determined that an upgraded system within the customer service department will yield a 3 percent reduction in costs. Even though the focus of this specific strategic execution is within the customer services department, it becomes inherently everyone's responsibility to make sure the execution is successful and to assist as needed.

However, because the Dynamic Execution system incorporates an integrated feedback loop structure, a broad base of staff already has awareness, understanding, and involvement in this initiative.

You will come to recognize when we discuss the detailed steps associated with the Dynamic Execution core activities process that, even though it might appear to be a significant commitment of resources, it is an extremely efficient, self-generating, time-saving, and more cost-effective method of accomplishing an organization's objectives.

Because responsibilities, time commitments, and expectations are predefined, there is a much more efficient utilization of staff resources. Staff members are more willing to participate because they feel they are a part of the process. Remember, there is an up-front recognition and accommodation that these efforts will require some of their time, and there is a feeling of empowerment because they have been embedded into the processes.

Because internal staff is integrated into the process early on and remains involved throughout, there tends to be a significant reduction in the use of outside resources.

In addition, major benefits derive from the fact that staff understanding, knowledge, and training regarding the new systems, processes, and procedures resulting from the execution of the strategic initiative are also inherently embedded into the process.

Consider this. Involvement and communications through the feedback loops provide staff with an up-front understanding of the drivers behind the objectives and strategic initiatives. Involvement in determining the requirements of a new strategy, which, in turn, determines the disconnects, creates an understanding of how things work and why. The execution of tasks to close disconnects leads to an understanding of what needs to change and why.

The result is that by the time the strategic execution has been executed, the staff already has a comprehensive understanding of the why, when, how, and who of the new systems, processes, and procedures. This leads to reduced training costs and the ability to make immediate utilization and obtain successful output.

Both represent a significant improvement in the efficient use of staff resources, together with substantial cost savings and reductions in the time of execution.

Step One: Leveraging Knowledge Associated With The Creation Of Executive Objectives

Figure 14.1

Core Activity – Executive Objective

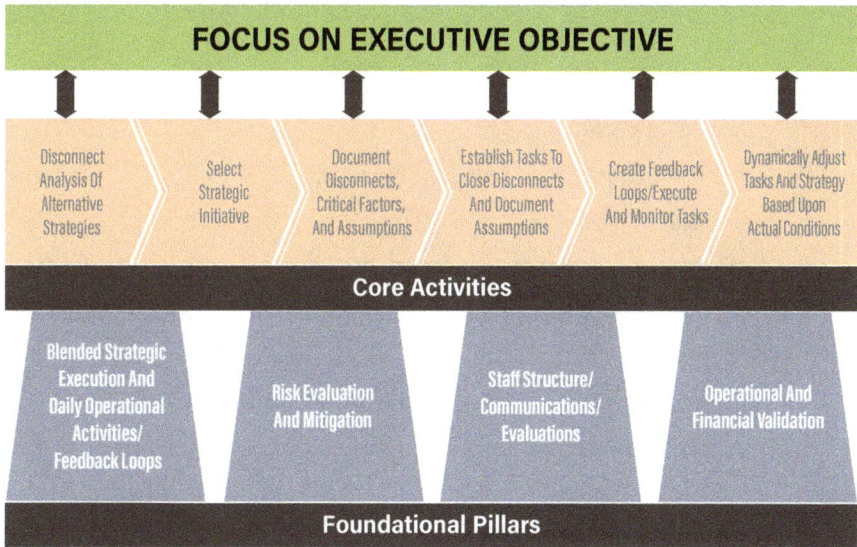

FOCUS ON EXECUTIVE OBJECTIVE

| Disconnect Analysis Of Alternative Strategies | Select Strategic Initiative | Document Disconnects, Critical Factors, And Assumptions | Establish Tasks To Close Disconnects And Document Assumptions | Create Feedback Loops/Execute And Monitor Tasks | Dynamically Adjust Tasks And Strategy Based Upon Actual Conditions |

Core Activities

| Blended Strategic Execution And Daily Operational Activities/ Feedback Loops | Risk Evaluation And Mitigation | Staff Structure/ Communications/ Evaluations | Operational And Financial Validation |

Foundational Pillars

The leveraging of information available from the decision-making process associated with the establishment of C-suite objectives is almost always a major missed opportunity.

This information not only signifies a vast number of critical criteria that can be used in the determination and selection of strategic initiatives but also represents an opportunity to significantly reduce the timeline associated with the accomplishment of the objectives.

My intent here is not to discuss the countless approaches promoted in the marketplace for the creation of executive goals and objectives.

Dynamic Execution can be effective irrespective of how executive objectives are established.

In fact, Dynamic Execution will help executives validate and, when necessary, efficiently and effectively modify their objectives.

However, I do want to stress that no matter what approach is used in determining executive objectives, there is critical information that is either consciously or subconsciously used during the decision-making process.

As highlighted in figure 14.2, this information includes the consideration of:

- Existing external and internal conditions. For example, there is X amount of total capacity available.
- External and internal drivers. For example, new customer demand will exceed available capacity.
- External and internal opportunities. For example, a competitor has had a major long-term disruption in their available capacity.
- Expected results if an objective is executed. For example, revenue will increase by $X if the objective to increase capacity is obtained.
- External and internal assumptions associated with the objective. For example, additional capacity will be obtained within six months.
- "When not if" considerations. For example, we have a high degree of certainty that demand will be increasing but the exact timing of the increase has a lot of uncertainty associated with it. Therefore, close monitoring must take place with consideration that (a) if capacity is added too early, we will jeopardize the availability of needed working capital, creating financial stress, and (b) if we

do not add capacity before demand begins, there is a risk of lost revenue and customer dissatisfaction.

As we will see next in step two of the core activities, the information documented during the creation of executive objectives becomes invaluable when determining and analyzing potential alternative strategies to accomplish these objectives.

For example, knowing expectations and assumptions represents a solid basis for the modeling and validation associated with each alternative strategy under consideration. And the understanding of the conditions, drivers, opportunities, and assumptions behind the objectives, along with any "when not if" considerations, represents vital fundamental information when analyzing the disconnects and any functionality trade-offs associated with each potential strategy.

In addition, the availability of all this information will help avoid confusion within the organization, act as a great basis for communication downward into the organization and feedback upward from the staff, and represent a detailed historical reference point when assessing if objectives are meeting expectations, or if modifications to these objectives should be considered due to the actual future external and internal dynamics that are taking place.

Finally, having this documented information jump-starts the execution process, thereby having a significant impact on reducing the timeline associated with accomplishing the objective.

Figure 14.2

Documentation Of Critical Information Used For Objective Decision-Making

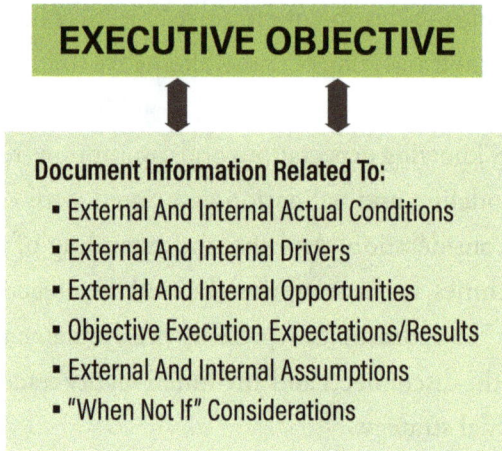

EXECUTIVE OBJECTIVE

Document Information Related To:
- External And Internal Actual Conditions
- External And Internal Drivers
- External And Internal Opportunities
- Objective Execution Expectations/Results
- External And Internal Assumptions
- "When Not If" Considerations

Summary of documented output from this step:

- Objective Description
- External And Internal Actual Conditions
- External And Internal Drivers
- External And Internal Opportunities
- Objective Execution Expectations/Results
- External And Internal Assumptions
- Target Date Considerations
- "When Not If" Considerations

Step Two: Analysis Of Alternative Strategies To Accomplish The Objective

Figure 14.3

Core Activity – Disconnect Analysis Of Alternative Strategies

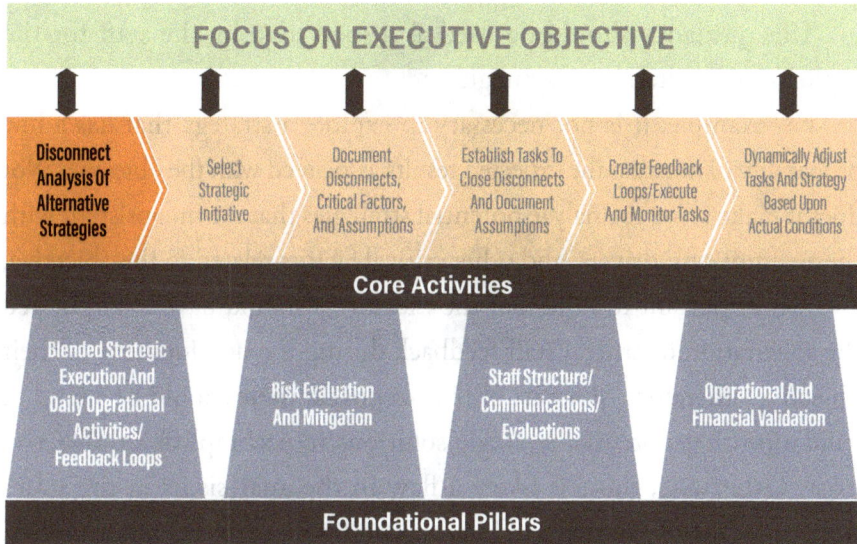

FOCUS ON EXECUTIVE OBJECTIVE

Disconnect Analysis Of Alternative Strategies

Select Strategic Initiative

Document Disconnects, Critical Factors, And Assumptions

Establish Tasks To Close Disconnects And Document Assumptions

Create Feedback Loops/Execute And Monitor Tasks

Dynamically Adjust Tasks And Strategy Based Upon Actual Conditions

Core Activities

Blended Strategic Execution And Daily Operational Activities/ Feedback Loops

Risk Evaluation And Mitigation

Staff Structure/ Communications/ Evaluations

Operational And Financial Validation

Foundational Pillars

As indicated in figures 5.3 and 5.4 in chapter 5, the primary responsibility for step one is with the C-suite/owners/senior executives.

In step two, the role of senior executives shifts to one of monitoring, oversight, and sign-off. This means that the primary responsibility for the development and analysis of alternative strategies to accomplish the objectives flows down into the organization and normally becomes the primary responsibility of junior executives and middle management such as directors and senior managers.

However, as indicated in figure 14.4, this development and analysis of potential alternative strategies is performed under a structured context.

Leveraging Of Information Associated With The Development Of The Objective

First, the information documented in step one during the development of the objective by the executives becomes a clear basis for providing guidance as to what the expectations are and what all the critical factors are that went into the creation of the objective.

This guidance should be used as a road map by the staff for the exploration of alternative strategies.

For example, it is not necessary to explore a strategy that has a low probability of meeting the expected results associated with the objective. Nor does it make sense to analyze potential strategies that are inconsistent with the assumptions, drivers, and other critical factors related to the objective.

It is important to note that the executives should have incorporated the solicitation of critical staff feedback during the development of their objective. Therefore, as a part of that feedback, there should be a level of validation that potential strategic solutions to accomplish an objective exist. Otherwise, there is likely a flaw in the analysis or in the staff's understanding of external and internal conditions, drivers, opportunities, or assumptions that needs to be addressed.

Disconnect Analysis

The second component of the structured approach for the development and analysis of potential alternative strategies is the use of disconnect analysis.

Determining the disconnects between the requirements associated with a given potential strategy and the actual conditions that exist within the organization is an extremely powerful tool when assessing the pros and cons of the various alternative strategies.

These disconnects provide an immediate high-level picture of the effort and challenges associated with any given potential strategy. In turn, there is an ability to quickly either eliminate or determine what further analysis is required for any given alternative.

Please note that in the vast majority of cases, just the determination of the disconnects provides a sufficient amount of information relative to an estimate of effort and resource requirements. In turn, this avoids at this point in the process the need to perform detailed analysis of the specific tasks to close a disconnect. The detailed analysis and creation of these tasks will generally only be performed on the final selected strategy.

I caution executives that RFQs and RFPs (request for quotes/request for proposals) or other such tools need to be handled with care. These sorts of exercises can turn into a proof of fit/concept both internally or on the part of the providers to promote their solutions. They tend to be functionality-oriented and even though they might meet a functionality requirement, as already discussed many times, under disconnect analysis, these solution sets can easily represent major execution issues. Even the "proven ones."

To avoid confusion, I am not saying that internal analysis of functionalities that might represent a strategic solution to accomplish an objective are not relevant. I am just raising caution to potential pitfalls that can exist when they are tied to RFQs, RFPs, or similar techniques used in the analytical assessment of solution sets in the marketplace.

Validation And Risk Analysis

Finally, the next two components of this structured approach are (a) a validation of the assumptions and expected results associated with a potential strategy, and (b) an assessment of any risks associated with a given potential strategy.

As discussed in chapter 12, the validation requires the integrated assessment by operations and finance that the assumptions and expected results associated with a potential strategy will meet or exceed the expectations established by the executives when they created the objective.

Once again, if there is an indication that a potential strategy does not meet the required expectations, that strategy needs to be modified, combined with other strategies, or eliminated.

The final analysis is one of the risks. Determine what the significant and/or high probability risks are, if any, associated with a given alternative strategy. Also, are these risks controllable, in which case, what are the potential effort and resources required to eliminate the risk? Or, are the risks uncontrollable; in which case, what are the potential effort and resources required to mitigate the risk?

Advanced Testing

This is a good point to introduce the benefits of advanced testing.

As part of the analysis of alternative strategies, there can be opportunities to perform advanced testing of such things as critical factors, assumptions, solution-set processes, or even the actual theory behind the alternative strategy under consideration.

When advanced testing is feasible, it cannot only help discover superior alternatives by validating their accuracy and applicability in advance but also lead to an ability to greatly reduce execution time and avoid potential issues.

Numerous times I was able to significantly reduce execution times of a successful objective by performing advanced testing of critical concepts, assumptions, and processes under consideration.

It should be noted that advanced testing is not only applicable during the analysis of alternative strategies but will be revisited when we discuss the establishment and execution of tasks for the strategy that is finally selected.

Figure 14.4

Analysis Of Strategic Solutions To Accomplish An Objective

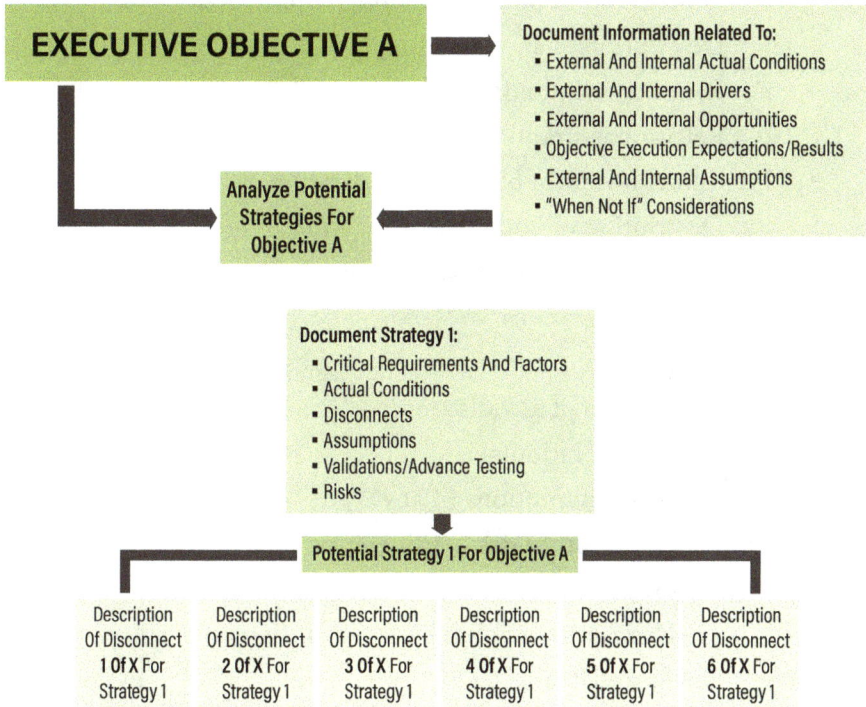

In the end, the documented output from step two for each potential strategy should include the following:

- Strategic description
- Disconnect analysis (one for each critical factor/requirement)
  - Critical requirement
  - Actual conditions
  - Description of disconnect (if a disconnect exists)
  - Required solution(s) (if any)
  - Relevant assumptions (if any)
- Functionality trade-off analysis
  - Description of any functionality trade-offs
  - Required solution(s)

- o Relevant assumptions (if any)
- High-level resource-to-disconnect considerations
  - o Description of potential staffing requirements
  - o Description of any disconnects
  - o Required solution(s)
  - o Relevant assumptions (if any)
- High-level review of budget considerations
  - o Description of budget considerations
  - o Relevant assumptions (if any)
- Timing considerations
  - o Description of timing considerations
  - o Description of any disconnects
  - o Required solution(s)
  - o Relevant assumptions (if any)
- Description of other risk considerations
  - o Controllable
    - Description of elimination plan (if any)
  - o Uncontrollable
    - Description of mitigation plan (if any)
  - o Relevant assumptions (if any)
- Operational/financial modeling and analytical validation
  - o Critical factors and assumptions used in the analysis
  - o Results of financial modeling and analytical validation
- When applicable, describe any advanced testing that has been or can be performed

Step Three: Selection And Documentation Of Strategy To Accomplish The Objective

Figure 14.5

Core Activities – Select Strategic Initiative And Document Disconnects, Critical Factors, And Assumptions

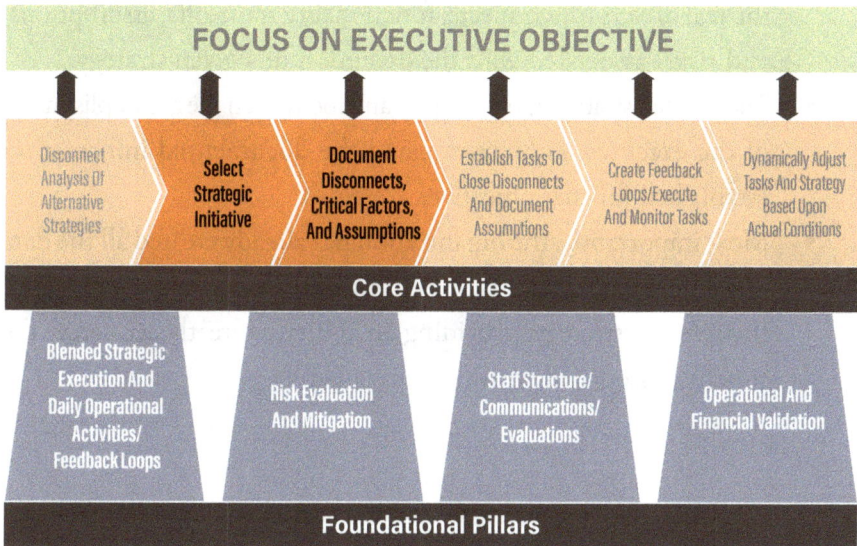

Step two provides the organization and executives with the information for each potential alternative strategy necessary to either make a selection of a strategy to execute or determine if additional analysis and effort is required before an initial selection is made.

Figure 14.6 depicts the beauty and power of the output created in step two for use in the step-three selection process.

- There is a consistent format, set of detailed information, and analytical review for each alternative strategy.
- Executives and staff can efficiently, effectively, and quickly understand and analyze all the critical data associated with each alternative strategy.

- Pro and con analysis across alternative strategies can efficiently, effectively, and quickly be created, analyzed, assessed, and discussed by the executives and staff.
- The final selection of a strategy is based upon actual data specific to the organization, avoiding marketplace generalizations, hidden execution exposures and risks, and the lack of understanding of the real drivers (disconnects, functionality trade-offs, assumptions, and risks) associated with the execution of a given strategy.
- The selected strategy is based upon and focused on the accomplishment of the executive's objective using the documented information established for that objective.
- Most importantly, the organization has already created all the data and information necessary to jump-start the actual execution of the selected strategy, providing an ability to greatly accelerate the timeline associated with the selected strategy.

Figure 14.6

Analysis Of Alternative Strategic Solutions To Accomplish Objective

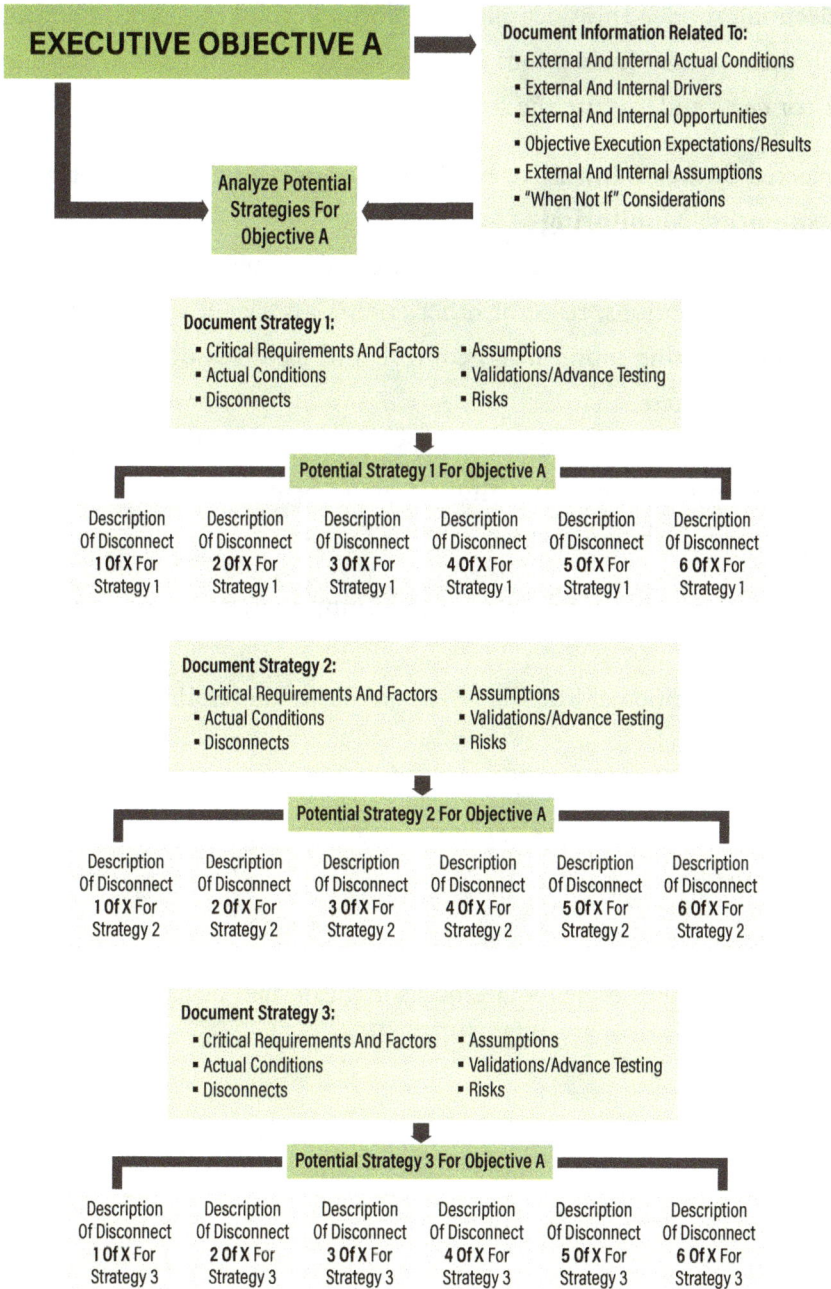

EXECUTIVE OBJECTIVE A

Document Information Related To:
- External And Internal Actual Conditions
- External And Internal Drivers
- External And Internal Opportunities
- Objective Execution Expectations/Results
- External And Internal Assumptions
- "When Not If" Considerations

Analyze Potential Strategies For Objective A

Document Strategy 1:
- Critical Requirements And Factors
- Actual Conditions
- Disconnects
- Assumptions
- Validations/Advance Testing
- Risks

Potential Strategy 1 For Objective A

| Description Of Disconnect 1 Of X For Strategy 1 | Description Of Disconnect 2 Of X For Strategy 1 | Description Of Disconnect 3 Of X For Strategy 1 | Description Of Disconnect 4 Of X For Strategy 1 | Description Of Disconnect 5 Of X For Strategy 1 | Description Of Disconnect 6 Of X For Strategy 1 |

Document Strategy 2:
- Critical Requirements And Factors
- Actual Conditions
- Disconnects
- Assumptions
- Validations/Advance Testing
- Risks

Potential Strategy 2 For Objective A

| Description Of Disconnect 1 Of X For Strategy 2 | Description Of Disconnect 2 Of X For Strategy 2 | Description Of Disconnect 3 Of X For Strategy 2 | Description Of Disconnect 4 Of X For Strategy 2 | Description Of Disconnect 5 Of X For Strategy 2 | Description Of Disconnect 6 Of X For Strategy 2 |

Document Strategy 3:
- Critical Requirements And Factors
- Actual Conditions
- Disconnects
- Assumptions
- Validations/Advance Testing
- Risks

Potential Strategy 3 For Objective A

| Description Of Disconnect 1 Of X For Strategy 3 | Description Of Disconnect 2 Of X For Strategy 3 | Description Of Disconnect 3 Of X For Strategy 3 | Description Of Disconnect 4 Of X For Strategy 3 | Description Of Disconnect 5 Of X For Strategy 3 | Description Of Disconnect 6 Of X For Strategy 3 |

Once a final strategy is selected, the documented information associated with that strategy from step two should be updated to reflect any additional analysis, data, and important discussions associated with the step-three selection process. This documented information for the selected strategy will then be used in step four for the establishment of tasks to close the disconnects and execute the strategic initiative.

Selected Strategic Initiative Feedback Loops And Critical Factor/Assumption Monitoring

Finally, there needs to be an assessment and documentation of any critical factors, assumptions, risks, or other criteria associated with the selected strategy requiring monitoring, control, and feedback during the actual execution process.

This documentation details the strategic initiative-level critical factor and assumption monitoring information to be used within the feedback loop system. It should include:

- Description of critical factors, assumptions, risks, or other criteria to monitor
- Description of who will be responsible for monitoring and providing feedback
- Description of timing to perform monitoring and feedback
- Description of the communication channel (who is included in the feedback loop)

At this point in the process, it is not unusual to focus on high-level documentation of these requirements that can then be used in steps four and five for a more detailed drilling down and incorporation into the execution.

During steps four and five, specific tasks can be established when needed, and critical monitoring/feedback criteria, analysis, and execution monitoring points can be created.

Step Four: Establish Tasks To Close Disconnects

Figure 14.7

Core Activity – Establish Tasks To Close Disconnects And Document Assumptions

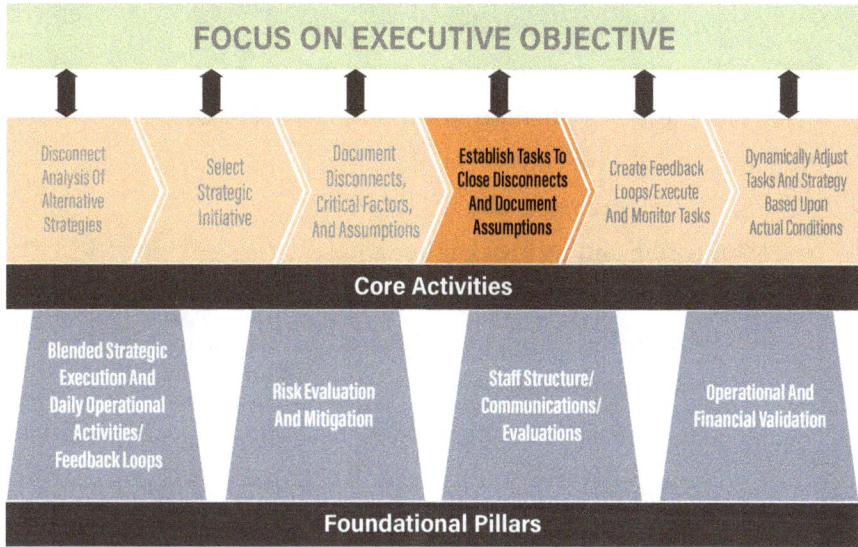

FOCUS ON EXECUTIVE OBJECTIVE

| Disconnect Analysis Of Alternative Strategies | Select Strategic Initiative | Document Disconnects, Critical Factors, And Assumptions | Establish Tasks To Close Disconnects And Document Assumptions | Create Feedback Loops/Execute And Monitor Tasks | Dynamically Adjust Tasks And Strategy Based Upon Actual Conditions |

Core Activities

| Blended Strategic Execution And Daily Operational Activities/ Feedback Loops | Risk Evaluation And Mitigation | Staff Structure/ Communications/ Evaluations | Operational And Financial Validation |

Foundational Pillars

The critical thing to note in this step four is that the focus should be on which tasks need to be executed in order to close each disconnect as efficiently and effectively as possible. In other words, the *why* has already been established in prior steps in the context of defined disconnects. Therefore, this step focuses on the *how* and by *whom* in the form of the required tasks necessary to close the disconnects.

The focus in this step is not the determination of the *when*. That will be addressed in more detail in chapter 15 on resource-to-disconnect analysis and dynamic scheduling.

As presented in figure 14.8, each disconnect will have its own set of required tasks and in turn, the following detailed information will also need to be determined and documented for each task:

- Disconnect and task reference numbers
- Task description
- Task resource-to-disconnect considerations
- Task budget considerations
- Task timing considerations
  - Determine nonsequential opportunities
  - Detail of sequential timing considerations
  - Detail any "when not if" timing considerations
- Specific task risk considerations
- Specific relevant task assumptions
- Monitoring and feedback criteria for the task
  - Description of criteria factors and/or assumptions to monitor
  - Description of who will be responsible for monitoring and providing feedback
  - Description of timing to perform monitoring and feedback
  - Description of communication channel (who is included in feedback loop)
- When applicable, a description of any advanced testing that has or can be performed relative to this task or group of tasks (this is consistent with the advanced testing described in step two for analysis of strategic alternatives)

It is, once again, important that the analysis and establishment of specific tasks are done within the context and boundaries of the prior documented information associated with the objective and documented information associated with the selected strategy.

Objective documented information:

- External and internal actual conditions
- External and internal drivers
- External and internal opportunities
- Expected objective results

- External and internal assumptions
- "When not if" considerations

Selected strategy documented information:

- Critical requirements and factors
- Actual conditions
- Disconnects
- Assumptions
- Validation/advance testing
- Risks
- Critical factors, assumptions, risks, or other criteria requiring monitoring, control, and feedback during the execution process (Established in step three)

Finally, as highlighted in figure 14.8, the number of tasks required, type of task, configuration, and associativity between the tasks essential to close a given disconnect will be unique to that particular disconnect and organization.

Therefore, while there can be similarities and even duplications of tasks for a common solution between two different organizations, the actual tasks will be influenced based upon the characteristics, structure, and operations of each specific organization. In other words, a major advantage of Dynamic Execution is that all aspects of a strategic execution are based upon the actual conditions and characteristics associated with an executive's specific organization. This then drives the actual disconnects and required tasks to close those disconnects to be unique to that organization.

Figure 14.8

Establish Tasks To Close Disconnects And Execute Selected Strategy

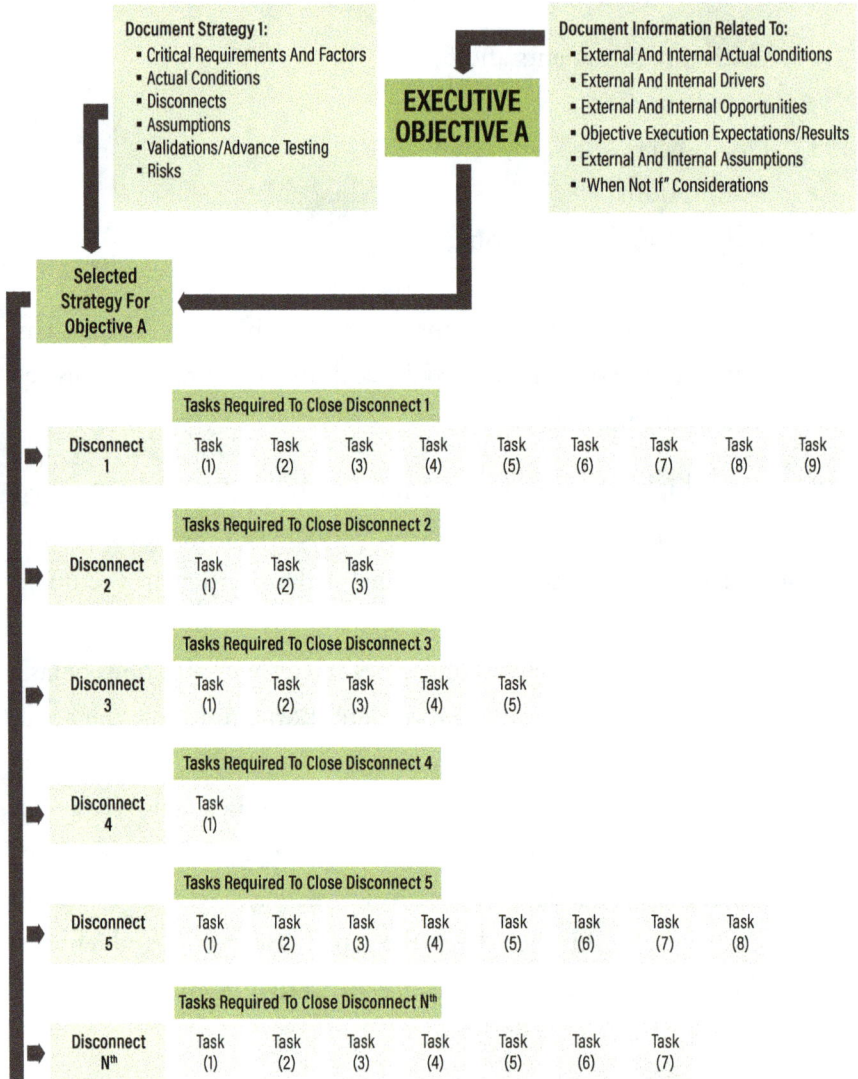

Document Strategy 1:
- Critical Requirements And Factors
- Actual Conditions
- Disconnects
- Assumptions
- Validations/Advance Testing
- Risks

EXECUTIVE OBJECTIVE A

Document Information Related To:
- External And Internal Actual Conditions
- External And Internal Drivers
- External And Internal Opportunities
- Objective Execution Expectations/Results
- External And Internal Assumptions
- "When Not If" Considerations

Selected Strategy For Objective A

Tasks Required To Close Disconnect 1

Disconnect 1	Task (1)	Task (2)	Task (3)	Task (4)	Task (5)	Task (6)	Task (7)	Task (8)	Task (9)

Tasks Required To Close Disconnect 2

Disconnect 2	Task (1)	Task (2)	Task (3)

Tasks Required To Close Disconnect 3

Disconnect 3	Task (1)	Task (2)	Task (3)	Task (4)	Task (5)

Tasks Required To Close Disconnect 4

Disconnect 4	Task (1)

Tasks Required To Close Disconnect 5

Disconnect 5	Task (1)	Task (2)	Task (3)	Task (4)	Task (5)	Task (6)	Task (7)	Task (8)

Tasks Required To Close Disconnect N^{th}

Disconnect N^{th}	Task (1)	Task (2)	Task (3)	Task (4)	Task (5)	Task (6)	Task (7)

15

Deep Dive Into Dynamic Execution Core Activities
Steps Five And Six

I n steps one through four, core activities must be performed and the output must be created in a structured context. This structured context provides two main benefits.

Structured Context Benefit One:
Learn/Document/Start Execution

First, the structured context provides a consistent basis to understand and document the significant information and dynamics for the accomplishment of executive objectives.

In addition, believe it or not, it also provides the capability to immediately and simultaneously start the execution process for the accomplishment of the objective.

In traditional strategic executions, project and implementation plans are generally created by a select group within the organization (often with significant assistance from external resources). Therefore, the actual execution starts when the project is launched.

This leaves much of the understanding of the *why, how, who*, and *when* by the broader staff in the organization to take place after the project launch (i.e., part of the purpose of the launch meeting).

Under Dynamic Execution, organization-wide staff involvement in steps one through four is immediate, thereby creating a simultaneous and instantaneous start to the strategic execution.

In turn, this leads to a significant reduction in the timeline associated with the accomplishment of executive objectives. It is just intrinsically more efficient and effective.

For example, in step one, all the drivers, conditions, opportunities, and assumptions used by executive management to establish their objectives/expectations are documented and shared. This creates the platform to solicit feedback and teach the organization the *why* behind the decisions made.

In essence, executives have already started the execution process by driving the organization to start thinking about critical factors, potential solutions, opportunities, and dynamics before strategies for objectives have even begun to be selected.

Therefore, by the completion of step four, everything about the strategic execution is known, understood, available, and disseminated to the staff regarding the *why, how*, and *who*.

There is a clear focus on only those efforts required to execute the strategy and obtain the objective. That is the execution of the tasks to close the disconnects. This leads to superior staff participation and execution. Once again, there will be a reduction in the timeline to execute and obtain the objective.

Structured Context Benefit Two: Consistency Across Staff

The second benefit to the structure associated with steps one through four is that the execution of Dynamic Execution core activities operates across a staff having varying levels of background, training, responsibilities, involvement, and motivations.

I know many individuals who like to skip ahead and backtrack only if necessary. I, too, at times, like to accelerate a process by trying to assemble a new toy without looking at the directions.

However, consistency of process in steps one through four generates (a) an improved ability for staff with varying characteristics and capabilities to learn and execute the process, (b) an ability to obtain consistent output from the process, and (c) a consistent set of staff expectations relative to responsibilities, involvement, and output.

Step Five And Step Six: A Hybrid Structure

Figure 15.1

Core Activities - Create Feedback Loops / Execute And Monitor Tasks / Dynamically Adjust Tasks And Strategy Based Upon Actual Conditions

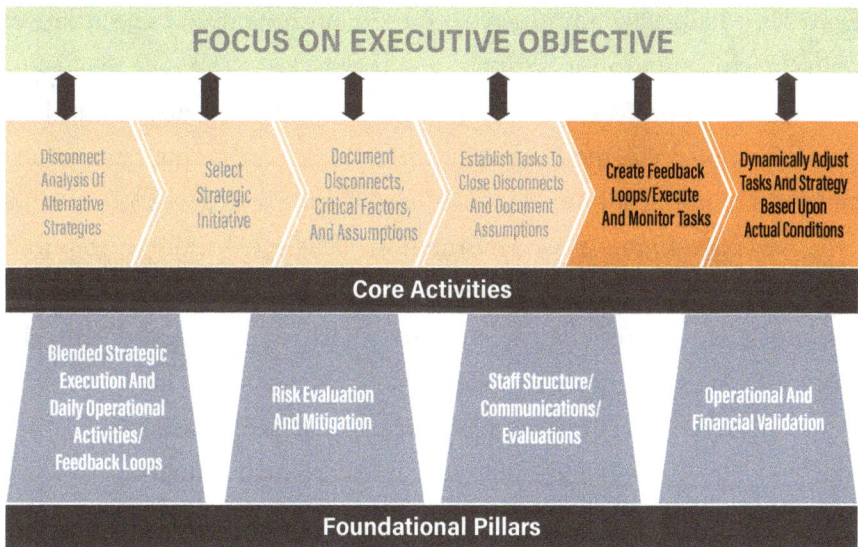

FOCUS ON EXECUTIVE OBJECTIVE					
Disconnect Analysis Of Alternative Strategies	Select Strategic Initiative	Document Disconnects, Critical Factors, And Assumptions	Establish Tasks To Close Disconnects And Document Assumptions	Create Feedback Loops/Execute And Monitor Tasks	Dynamically Adjust Tasks And Strategy Based Upon Actual Conditions

Core Activities

Blended Strategic Execution And Daily Operational Activities/ Feedback Loops	Risk Evaluation And Mitigation	Staff Structure/ Communications/ Evaluations	Operational And Financial Validation

Foundational Pillars

In step five and step six I shift gears to a hybrid approach to the execution of Dynamic Execution core activities.

Step five is a continuation of a structured approach that includes (a) the creation and execution of the monitoring, control, feedback, and management of critical factors and (b) activities associated with the analysis and modification, if any, to tasks and strategies.

However, with regard to the actual scheduling and execution of specific tasks, there needs to be a recognition that the organization is operating in a daily/weekly/monthly environment that is much more dynamic—an environment with accelerated changing conditions for both operational and strategic execution activities.

Therefore, in step six, I will discuss a dynamic structure that will be used for the scheduling and actual execution of core activities. This will include resource-to-disconnect analysis and dynamic scheduling.

Step Five: Create Feedback Loops, Monitor Tasks, And Adjust As Needed

Monitoring/Control/Feedback Points

The output/documentation available from step three and step four already provides a kick-start advantage to the establishment and execution of critical factor monitoring, control, and feedback.

Strategic initiative–level information for selected strategy: step three documentation details the strategic initiative–level critical factors, assumptions, and risk monitoring information to be used within the feedback loop system.

Disconnect and task-level information for selected strategy: step four documentation details the disconnect- and task-level critical factors, assumptions, and risk-monitoring information to be used within the feedback loop system.

Therefore, the following information is already available for both *strategic initiative level* and *disconnect* and *task level* information:

- Description of criteria factors, assumptions, risks, or other criteria to monitor
- Description of who will be responsible for monitoring and providing feedback
- Description of timing to perform monitoring and feedback

- Description of the communication channel (who is included in the feedback loop)

Note: You will see in figure 15.3 that the task-level monitoring and feedback information will be incorporated into the resource-to-disconnect analysis scheduling information.

However, while the strategic-level monitoring and feedback requirements can also be incorporated within the resource-to-disconnect analysis scheduling system, I prefer to keep the strategic-level activities in an independent context. I find an independent context is cleaner and less confusing. It is easier to manage and more flexible when controlled independently.

As indicated in chapter 5, figures 5.3 and 5.4, depending on the size of the organization and its hierarchical management structure, the primary responsibility to use this information for the actual establishment and oversight of both strategic-level and task-level monitoring and feedback activities falls to the directors, senior managers, and/or managers. This allocation of responsibility is logical given that this same group had primary responsibility for the generation of this documented information during steps three and four.

Resolution Analysis And Recommendations For Detected Issues

Like statistical process control used in operations, the monitoring and feedback for strategic execution should be ongoing and consistently occurring.

It is important to recognize that these monitoring and feedback activities are independent of the timing for executing the actual tasks.

In other words, it is important to continuously understand the status of all critical factors and risks throughout the entire execution process via the monitoring and feedback system. While the execution of a given task might negatively affect these conditions, in reality, there will be a much broader set of dynamics continuously taking place that can negatively affect critical factors and risks. Therefore, the monitoring taking place at the time of a specific task execution will just be integrated into this broader ongoing monitoring process.

If any deviations or issues are detected, they should be immediately addressed, and a determination should be made as to any remedial actions that might be required.

Once again, the execution of this resolution analysis and development of any recommendations falls within the responsibilities of directors, senior managers, and/or managers of the organization. However, feedback regarding the discovery and analysis of any detected issues should also be immediately communicated to the organization and executive management.

In addition, any modifications to the previous strategy and execution plans signed off by executives must be once again approved and signed off by executive management.

Step Six: Scheduling And Execution Of Tasks

There is no doubt that the management of resources and scheduling of the execution of strategic tasks can be among the more challenging of the core activities within Dynamic Execution.

As noted above, these activities are taking place in an environment with accelerated changing conditions for both operational and strategic execution activities—for example, continuously changing demand for products and services, continuously changing staff availability, and continuously changing availability of other resources.

Scheduling and execution of strategic activities must be performed simultaneously with operational activities within a blended organizational structure.

The existing systems in place to schedule operational activities can already vary significantly from organization to organization due to such things as differing types of product and service offerings, administration versus production/service offering activities, size of the organization, management and operational philosophies, and established systems, processes, procedures, and methodologies.

Therefore, I will not provide a single methodology that will automatically apply to any organization. However, I will provide a set of concepts, tools, and techniques that will assist and can be universally utilized in the scheduling and execution of tasks in a blended organizational structure.

Solving Complexity Is Not Impossible

It is critical to recognize that the existence of complex scheduling systems for operating activities is not uncommon.

Illustration: An organization was a major player in the manufacturing and sale of urethane load wheels.

These wheels were of various sizes and configurations and were manufactured by pouring liquid urethane into a mold that held a metal hub that was coated with a bonding agent. The mold was composed of multiple pieces of tooling assembled to create the exact size and configuration of the end product.

To complicate things, many of the tooling pieces used to assemble the required mold for a given end product were not unique to that product. Instead, they could be used in the assembly of multiple molds for multiple end products.

On any given day, (a) there was a demand for multiple end products in multiple quantities, (b) the bonding agent applied to the metal hubs took twenty-four hours to cure and had to then be used within forty-eight hours before it was no longer viable, (c) there were a finite number of any given tooling, which, in turn, added significant complexity by limiting the number and quantity of different molds/end products that could be produced in any given time period, and (d) not only were there differences in the molds, but different customers could also require different types of urethanes.

Therefore, the ability to effectively schedule and meet customer shipping requirements was incredibly complex and almost impossible to comprehend.

However, the actual manufacturing process had at least been automated and consisted of a continuous circular-flow production line.

A scheduled product was manufactured by assembling the mold based on the required pieces of tooling and inserting a hub into the mold. The assembled mold traveled along a moving belt to a holding area for the urethane pouring machine, and it was then filled. After filling, the mold traveled into a curing oven where the urethane cured as it traveled in the oven along the belt. The cured final product emerged from the oven, was manually demolded, and the finished product was placed on a finished goods rack. The disassembled mold tooling pieces traveled back to the first mold assembly station to either be immediately used again or removed and set aside for future use.

It should be noted that every time the urethane pouring machine stopped pouring, it had to be purged of any urethane remaining in the pour tube (which represented very costly waste) before the next mold could be filled. Therefore, the ability to continually fill molds without stopping represented a significant cost-saving opportunity.

There was significant growth in demand for these products and I was tasked with determining how the organization could improve production efficiency and take advantage of any cost-reduction opportunities (such as a reduction in the waste incurred due to the purging at the urethane pour station).

The solution lay in creating an ability to *dynamically determine/schedule* what product was most critical to produce when, in what quantities, and in a continuous flow to meet on-time delivery while maximizing throughput with effective tool utilization.

In other words, an objective was established that the urethane pouring machine would continuously run at a known flow rate (thereby minimizing waste). Therefore, incoming customer orders could be analyzed based on the pour time (urethane consumption) required to complete the orders (matching a condition to a requirement), which also then determined the tooling requirements for each order.

We could then use the pour time and tooling-requirements data (i.e., requirements) to dynamically populate time slots (i.e., match actual conditions to the requirements) on the production line.

These populated time slots balanced the line to support a continuous flow and avoided any conflicts between products that utilized overlapping tooling but would still fulfill on-time delivery.

The bottom line is that throughput was increased by more than ten times, and waste was reduced by more than 90 percent, all without the need to add any additional equipment or tooling.

I use this long illustration because it represents an extremely complex scheduling and execution challenge that was solved using Dynamic Execution concepts, including dynamic scheduling and execution.

It clearly reinforces that even though the execution of a strategic initiative can be complex, a clear understanding of assumptions, requirements, conditions, and tasks, along with dynamic scheduling and execution, represent a superior way to obtain success.

Dynamic Scheduling Considerations And Objectives

As highlighted in figure 15.2, some considerations and objectives need to be incorporated into dynamic scheduling of strategic execution activities.

Foremost, scheduling must be integrated/blended with the scheduling of operational requirements. However, that does not mean that the execution of strategic activities is subservient to the execution of operational activities. The objective must be to efficiently and effectively accomplish the execution of both sets of activities.

There should be an ability to execute multiple strategic executions simultaneously.

There should be an ability to dynamically throttle strategic execution activities based upon the monitoring and feedback of actual conditions and "when not if" considerations.

Finally, there should be an ability to dynamically adjust the scheduling and execution of strategic activities based upon continuous resource-to-disconnect monitoring.

Figure 15.2

Dynamic Execution

Provides Ability To Simultaneously Execute Multiple Objectives

Execution Efforts And Timing For Each Objective Are Throttled
Based Upon Monitoring And Feedback Of Actual Conditions To Assumptions

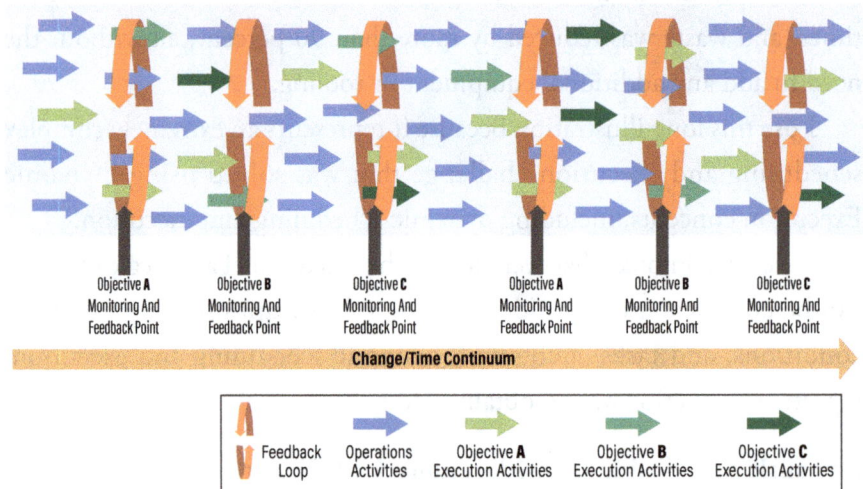

| Objective **A** Monitoring And Feedback Point | Objective **B** Monitoring And Feedback Point | Objective **C** Monitoring And Feedback Point | Objective **A** Monitoring And Feedback Point | Objective **B** Monitoring And Feedback Point | Objective **C** Monitoring And Feedback Point |

Change/Time Continuum

| Feedback Loop | Operations Activities | Objective **A** Execution Activities | Objective **B** Execution Activities | Objective **C** Execution Activities |

Resource-To-Disconnect Analysis And Dynamic Scheduling

To once again state the obvious, not all requirements associated with a strategic initiative are equal.

Some are foundational and need to exist before certain other requirements can be obtained. The execution of some requirements can occur simultaneously (i.e., independent of the timing and execution of other tasks). Also, the amount of time, effort, capability, and resources utilized in establishing the various critical requirements can vary significantly.

In a traditional execution methodology, you create a plan, launch it, and plow your way through it until completion, which I like to refer to as a linear fashion.

Traditional approaches tend to assume that adequate financial, staff, and other resources are automatically available when needed and ignore other dynamics that might be taking place.

Those approaches entail more of a laser-like focus on just sequentially completing the implementation plan on a preestablished timeline for the accomplishment of a forced set of requirements.

The alternative I prefer begins with a disconnect analysis that details which specific requirements are missing from the conditions that currently exist.

These disconnects are then further analyzed to determine specific time, effort, capability, and other resource requirements for each disconnect along with significance, interrelationships, and potential sequential positioning considerations.

This analysis becomes the basis for dynamically scheduling the execution of strategic initiatives, which in turn provides a clear understanding of the availability and timing of required resources.

Similar to the urethane illustration above, this approach creates an ability to dynamically determine which strategic initiatives are the most critical to focus on and when, using which resources, and in an execution flow that meets the desired objectives when actually needed.

All execution is in a blended context with operational activities, thereby minimizing any disruptions to operations.

This approach also addresses the pitfalls in a "when not if" execution through selective execution of disconnects that prepare for rapid deployment once the "when" is finally determined. Therefore, critical resources can be controlled and preserved until they are absolutely needed.

Note that this approach helps recognize how certain major disconnects can be broken down into smaller efforts that create the ability to have a rapid deployment while preserving critical resources.

Dynamic Execution creates the ability to simultaneously execute multiple strategic initiatives while effectively shifting priorities and resources based on any changing dynamics that are taking place.

It also creates an ability to leverage the structure of feedback-loop assumption and condition monitoring, allowing the capability to quickly adjust the execution process, priorities, or strategic direction.

While it might appear that this methodology represents a lot of effort and will slow the execution down, it, in fact, is just the opposite, and execution time is actually significantly reduced.

Resource-To-Disconnect Analysis

What is resource-to-disconnect analysis?

It is the structuring of all the data and information developed and documented in steps one through four in a framework that supports the analysis and communication necessary for the efficient and effective execution of strategic activities.

I recognize that all sorts of project management and control systems are already available and in use.

While I am not totally averse to many of these alternative project management/scheduling systems and their potential use, I do think in most situations they can be overkill and a simple spreadsheet database structure will be as good if not better.

However, my objective here is not to explore the pros and cons of project management systems.

Instead, my objective is to communicate how the documented data created within the Dynamic Execution system can be formatted, analyzed, and efficiently and effectively utilized for the blended scheduling and execution of strategic activities.

In this context, I will come at it here from a simplified spreadsheet database structure.

Given the broad familiarity with this sort of spreadsheet tool, it allows for an easier and quicker grasp of functionality associated with sorting, summarizing, and presentation in order to perform alternative types of analysis, communication, and actionable activities.

The power and beauty of the resource-to-disconnect analysis is that it is simply a walk across of the information and data already created and documented in steps one through step four.

There is no need to put any additional effort into the creation of implementation and execution plans. All those efforts have already been accomplished. This greatly reduces the timeline associated with the accomplishment of the executive's objective.

Figure 15.3 is a table that summarizes (a) the information/data available to walk across from the documentation established in steps one through four, (b) a brief explanation of the information, and (c) how this information can be applied to scheduling activities.

The key is to visualize each line item included in this figure as a column in a resource-to-disconnect analysis spreadsheet.

Under this row/column structure, each row in the spreadsheet represents a single objective/strategy/disconnect/task relationship that can now be sorted, analyzed, and communicated in multiple configurations. Each configuration will serve all types of powerful functional applications and scheduling capabilities.

For example, if you sort by objective/strategy/disconnect/task, you will immediately display every objective by strategy, including individual disconnects for each selected strategy broken out and required tasks (see figure 14.8). If you include the task status and target date for each task in this sort, you can immediately determine the overall status of any given objective, strategy, and/or disconnect.

If you sort by department/functional area/group/status, you can immediately determine the open demand for resources for each department, functional area, and group. If you include target date (by either full date, year, month, or week), this demand on resources can be summarized by timing. If you include staff in the sort, you can determine demand by staff by timing or by timing by staff.

If you sort by staff/status/date/task, you can immediately determine the open demand for each individual staff member's involvement by date and task.

I could keep going, but I am sure you understand the analytical and scheduling power associated with this database of information and its associated sorting capability.

Before I move on to discussing dynamic scheduling in more detail, I do want to make sure as executives, you recognize this resource-to-disconnect analysis capability supports all of the objectives outlined below:

- Provides a clear understanding regarding the availability and timing of required resources
- Represents the ability to support simultaneous execution of multiple objectives
- Provides an ability to coordinate "when not if" considerations through selective execution of disconnects and tasks that prepare for rapid deployment once the "when" is finally determined
- Creates an ability to quickly adjust the data contained within the resource-to-disconnect analysis based upon any monitoring and feedback requirements and will inherently and immediately communicate these changes to all staff

Finally, while I find this data structure and use of spreadsheets powerful, there are obviously alternative formats and additional data that can be incorporated.

As already discussed, one can also infuse this into an existing system or structure currently in use.

However, as I have constantly pointed out, Dynamic Execution is an integrated and closed-loop system. Therefore, there can be major risk in deviation from the approaches and techniques I have presented.

While adding additional data information can be less risky and even beneficial, very careful consideration must be given to where this information will come from, in what context, and for what benefit.

Consideration for a focus on objective management and speed of execution built into Dynamic Execution should always be paramount.

Figure 15.3

Resource-To-Disconnect Analysis
Data/Information Requirements

DATA DESCRIPTION	EXPLANATION	APPLICATION
WHAT		
Objective Reference	Common Reference Control System	Key Field For Sorting And Data Referencing/Accumulation/Analysis
Objective Description	Recognizable Description Of Objective	Quick Reference Information For Staff
Strategy Reference	Common Reference Control System	Key Field For Sorting And Data Referencing/Accumulation/Analysis
Strategy Description	Recognizable Description Of Strategy	Quick Reference Information For Staff
Disconnect Reference	Common Reference Control System	Key Field For Sorting And Data Referencing/Accumulation/Analysis
Disconnect Description	Recognizable Description Of Disconnect	Quick Reference Information For Staff
Task Reference	Common Reference Control System	Key Field For Sorting And Data Referencing/Accumulation/Analysis
Task Description	Recognizable Description Of Task	Quick Reference Information For Staff
Expected Output From Task	Description/Location Of Required Output To Delineate Completion	Provides Staff With Required Output And Expectations
Current Status Of This Task	I.E. Open/Closed/In Progress/ Requires Resolution	Sort By Status For Scheduling/ Analysis/Control
Date Of Last Status Update	Date Above Status Was Last Updated	Quick Control Reference Information For Staff

DATA DESCRIPTION	EXPLANATION	APPLICATION
WHO		
Department	Applicable Area(s) Or Individual(s) Responsible For Execution	Sort By Responsibility For Scheduling/Analysis/Control
Functional Area	Applicable Area(s) Or Individual(s) Responsible For Execution	Sort By Responsibility For Scheduling/Analysis/Control
Group	Applicable Area(s) Or Individual(s) Responsible For Execution	Sort By Responsibility For Scheduling/Analysis/Control
Specific Staff Member	Applicable Area(s) Or Individual(s) Responsible For Execution	Sort By Responsibility For Scheduling/Analysis/Control
Primary Report Staff	Staff Responsible For Primary Oversight	Staff Reference + Sort By Responsibility For Oversight
Data Control/Update Staff	Staff Responsible To Update And Maintain Data	Staff Reference + Sort By Responsibility For Data Entry/Control
HOW		
Instructions And Guidance	Description Or Location Of Documentation – How To Execute Task	Provides Critical Execution Information To Meet Expectations
Support Staff	Available Staff To Assist In Understanding Execution Of Task	Provides Available Staff Information To Assist In Understanding
Advanced Testing Performed/ Opportunities	Description Of Any Advance Testing Performed Or Available	Represents Opportunity To Avoid Risk And Accelerate Execution
WHEN		
Target Date Of Task	Full Date Of Expected Required Task Completion	Sort By Date And Who For Scheduling/Analysis/Control
Target Year	Year Only Expected Required Task Completion	Sort By Date And Who For Scheduling/Analysis/Control
Target Month	Month Only Expected Required Task Completion	Sort By Date And Who For Scheduling/Analysis/Control
Target Week	Week Only Expected Required Task Completion	Sort By Date And Who For Scheduling/Analysis/Control
Sequential (Yes Or No)	Is This Task Part Of A Group Of Tasks Requiring Sequential Execution	Flexible/Accelerated Scheduling Of Nonsequential Tasks
If Sequential Prior Task Requiring Completion	Reference Of Task That Must Be Completed Before This Task	Scheduling/Sorting/Analysis/Control Of Sequential Tasks

DATA DESCRIPTION	EXPLANATION	APPLICATION
Target Date For Prior Task Completion	Date Prior Task Is Expected To Be Completed	Scheduling/Sorting/Analysis/Control Of Sequential Tasks
Prior Task Status	I.e. Open/Closed/In Progress/ Requires Resolution	Scheduling/Sorting/Analysis/Control Of Sequential Tasks
If Sequential Next Task After Completion	Reference Of Task That Must Be Completed After This Task	Scheduling/Sorting/Analysis/Control Of Sequential Tasks
Required By Date For Next Task	Date Next Task Is Expected To Start	Scheduling/Sorting/Analysis/Control Of Sequential Tasks
Interdependent On Other Nonsequential Tasks (Yes Or No)	Is This Task Interdependent On Any Other Nonsequential Task(s)	Scheduling/Sorting/Analysis/Control Of Interdependent Tasks
Description Of Interdependent Information/Task(s)	Description Of Interdependencies	Scheduling/Sorting/Analysis/Control Of Interdependent Tasks
Reference Numbers Of Interdependent Task(s)	Cross-References Of Other Task(s)	Scheduling/Sorting/Analysis/Control Of Interdependent Tasks
Required By Or After Date(s) For Interdependent Task(s)	Completion/Availability Dates Between Interdependent Task(s)	Scheduling/Sorting/Analysis/Control Of Interdependent Tasks
Monitoring Critical Task Criteria And Risk		
Description Of Critical Criteria	Description Of Critical Factors Requiring Monitoring And Feedback	What – Provides Staff With Required Information And Expectations
Timing Of Critical Criteria Monitoring	Description Of How Often And When Monitoring Needs To Occur	When – Provides Staff With Required Information And Expectations
Staff Responsible For Monitoring Critical Criteria	Description Of Staff Responsible For Monitoring And Feedback	Who – Provides Staff With Required Information And Expectations
Feedback Channel For Critical Criteria (I.e. Group Email Link)	Oversight Staff Receiving Feedback From Critical Factor Monitoring	Feedback Channel – Provides Staff With Required Information
Description Of Risk	Description Of Risk(s) Requiring Monitoring And Feedback	What – Provides Staff With Required Information And Expectations
Timing Of Risk Monitoring	Description Of How Often And When Risk Monitoring Needs To Occur	When – Provides Staff With Required Information And Expectations
Staff Responsible For Monitoring Risk	Description Of Staff Responsible For Risk Monitoring And Feedback	Who – Provides Staff With Required Information And Expectations
Feedback Channel For Risk (I.e. Group Email Link)	Oversight Staff Receiving The Feedback From Risk Monitoring	Feedback Channel – Provides Staff With Required Information

Dynamic Scheduling: Potential Challenges

By now, dynamically scheduling strategic activities in a blended context should be somewhat apparent.

The analytical and communication capabilities inherent within the configuration of the resource-to-disconnect analysis provide all the information required to schedule strategic activities all the way down to the staffing level of the individual.

If challenges exist, they tend to be associated with the integration of these execution activities with operational activities.

I have found there are two primary ways to address these challenges. One is attempting to integrate the strategic execution requirements into the existing operations scheduling structure. The other is providing the relevant information contained in the resource-to-disconnect analysis directly to the staff and empowering them to accomplish the requirements with the ability to recognize and address any concerns when needed.

I have determined the incorporation of both strategic and operations activities into a common scheduling system, while feasible, can be very difficult. It is usually more feasible in larger organizations. It is highly dependent on the type of organization and type of products and services being provided.

Because executive objectives and strategies almost always require organization-wide involvement, rarely is there a single organization-wide scheduling system. Attempts to incorporate the scheduling of both sets of activities into a common, highly structured system almost always leads to multiple scheduling systems across the various functional areas. This then generates the need to integrate and synchronize these multiple systems.

Consideration for a focus on objective management and speed of execution built into Dynamic Execution should not be sacrificed.

The benefits of the use of Dynamic Execution can be almost immediate and, therefore, should not be lost while these integration activities are being explored or implemented.

Ironically, if after the launch of dynamic scheduling within an organization it is determined there are benefits that might be derived from such an integration, Dynamic Execution should be used for this analysis and these efforts. But execute dynamic scheduling immediately using the spreadsheet approach.

Dynamic Scheduling: Most Effective Approach

I have found that the best way to integrate strategic execution activities with daily operations activities is to drive these efforts to the lowest level possible in the organization.

In other words, if you have effectively created a blended organization structure, the staff already recognize their dual responsibilities. Therefore, the best way to accomplish the scheduling and execution of both activities is to directly empower the staff.

Many executives embrace the concept of empowerment but find it difficult to define and implement.

I define empowerment as creating a structure where pragmatic and vetted information is disseminated to the staff so that decisions and execution can be performed at the lowest staffing level possible while still having access to immediate support when needed.

The ability to support staff empowerment is embedded within Dynamic Execution:

- Responsibilities are already clearly defined and communicated, and the time required for the execution of these efforts is recognized and accepted.
- Closed-loop organizational feedback loops establish bidirectional communication that supports the dissemination of information down into the organization and staff input up into the organization.
- As explained in chapter 5, including figures 5.3 and 5.4, a hierarchical staffing structure of responsibilities, involvement, and oversight inherently provides a support network that staff empowered with the execution of a task can leverage off of if and when needed.

Execution: Who/What/When/How

Answers to the *who/what/when/how* exist in the resource-to-disconnect analysis. So, the real question is how this information is used.

First, through the sorting and communication of the information within the resource-to-disconnect analysis, demand and timing can be summarized by department/functional area/group down to the individual staff level responsible for the execution.

Therefore, managers of these departments, functional areas, and groups have the continuous ability to monitor and analyze the strategic execution workload associated with their area of responsibility. This allows the managers and staff to dynamically integrate the execution of the strategic workload with the operations workload that exists at any point in time.

It is very important to note that this same management staff was involved (either directly or through feedback) during steps one through four in the creation of the strategic execution information and requirements. Therefore, they should already have a strong familiarity with both the details of this information and the associated requirements.

If there are potential issues or conflicts associated with the balancing of workloads between strategic and operations and/or in the ability to successfully execute the tasks, these issues should be immediately communicated, analyzed, resolved, and approved as described in step five (Create Feedback Loops, Monitor Tasks, And Adjust As Needed).

Finally, if there is an ongoing issue regarding the availability of staff resources, a reassessment of the time committed to strategic execution responsibilities should be performed. This reassessment does not necessarily lead to a need for additional resources. Instead, it often represents the need to adjust time commitments between existing staff, recognizing the training or knowledge of certain staff is better suited to strategic execution activities. In fact, I highly recommend that managers continually monitor these staffing dynamics in an effort to be preemptive in avoiding issues.

Remember, there is an ability to leverage the knowledge derived by managers during their involvement in steps one through four that will provide, in advance, the potential timing and amount of demand on departmental, functional area, and group staffing resources.

There is also the ability to explore and fine-tune the allocation of responsibilities during the innovative human resource methodologies discussed in chapter 11.

Provided below are available techniques that can provide flexibility in the scheduling and execution of strategic execution activities along with representing the potential to greatly reduce the timeline associated with the accomplishment of an objective.

Special Scheduling And Execution Technique One

I have already described how, when possible, advanced testing can be incredibly valuable.

I have seen advanced testing used throughout the Dynamic Execution process, even prior to the development and finalization of final executive objectives. Advanced testing allows executives and the organization to explore and validate, in a controlled context, the concepts, processes, and methodologies before making large commitments of focus, cost, and other resources.

It also creates an opportunity to accelerate the execution of strategies and the accomplishment of objectives. Executions are accelerated by developing a deeper assessment of critical requirements and conditions in addition to resolving potential critical issues prior to the broader commitment of organizational time and resources.

Special Scheduling And Execution Technique Two

Leveraging off of the timing of nonsequential versus sequential strategic execution activity represents an opportunity for significant benefits in the flexibility of scheduling, Dynamic Execution, and reduction of the overall execution timeline.

Nonsequential strategic activities provide staff with the ability to utilize time when it is available versus when the execution of a task has a stricter requirement associated with it. This capability can then open up the availability and flexibility of staff time in the future when the dynamics are less accommodating.

The only two cautions I raise are that careful consideration should be given when executing nonsequential tasks (a) that are known to have a high potential of modification or fine-tuning associated with them via the monitoring and feedback activities, and (b) in "when not if" situations, so large amounts of financial resources associated with the execution of these nonsequential activities are not prematurely committed. However, as we will now discuss, this consideration should be balanced in a broader context of potential opportunities associated with "when not if" scenarios.

Special Scheduling And Execution Technique Three

In cases where "when not if" considerations are at play, look for opportunities that position the organization for a rapid acceleration in the execution and completion of an objective should future dynamics call for it.

This could include the early execution of strategic activities such as critical tasks that have longer execution time requirements (especially those requiring a low commitment of financial resources), low-cost tasks, and technically difficult tasks.

Special Scheduling And Execution Technique Four

The simultaneous execution of multiple strategic initiatives provides an opportunity to utilize staffing when available instead of having to try to match availability with specific time periods.

For example, if demand for strategic execution in, say, period three exceeds available staff resources, look for opportunities across the entire spectrum of strategic initiatives for opportunities to pull forward some of those execution activities into periods one and two, where availability might be more accommodating.

The resource-to-disconnect analysis can be used as a master scheduling tool where analysis and balancing within the dynamic schedule can first be established in a broader context. From there, this master schedule is used to drive the detailed dynamic scheduling requirements down into the organization (i.e., departments, functional areas, groups, and individual staff) where the managers and staff are empowered to blend and execute the activities.

Remember that as an organization, there has been an assignment of responsibilities and the commitment of an established amount of staff time/resources to the execution of strategic activities.

If, through master scheduling analysis, it is determined strategic activity demand exceeds committed available staff resources, these conditions should be communicated to the executives, including possible solutions.

Therefore, the key is to use it wisely and in an efficient and effective way, that is a balanced blending with operational activities.

Do not lose the ability to reduce execution timelines and simultaneously accomplish multiple objectives because available resources are poorly coordinated.

The responsibility to coordinate and oversee these efforts resides with the directors, senior managers, and managers, who, in turn, are subject to the oversight of the executives.

Special Scheduling And Execution Technique Five

Migration of data can be a major driver of a long execution timeline. Historically, I used the following as my hidden migration technique to significantly reduce the launch of an objective.

It is common for the existing databases to be massive and complex and either contain information not included in the new database or be missing data required to exist in the new database.

Traditional implementations typically migrate and try to synchronize the data between the existing and newly required systems. This can take a tremendous amount of time to understand, map out, and migrate.

There is an often little-known and under-utilized trick that executives should be aware of before execution timelines are negatively affected by these efforts.

Rather than migrating all the data before the new systems or processes are fully launched, only migrate that data that is current and required immediately to support present operational requirements and efforts.

For example, it is not unusual for a customer master database to contain current and inactive or occasionally active customers.

Therefore, instead of migrating the entire database, focus the efforts on migrating only those customers who are currently active and maintain all other customer information in the original database, which can be used to update the new data on an as-needed basis (i.e., if an occasional customer places an order).

Even though I use the customer master database as an example, the same sort of process can often be utilized for vendor, inventory, and a multitude of accounting, engineering, and sales files.

When applicable, and it often is, the use of this sort of migration technique can significantly reduce the time associated with receiving the benefits from a fully executed objective.

Also note that in many cases, there is also a cost justification to maintain a portion of the old systems for a period of time in order to support historical analysis and/or an occasional/unexpected need for historical information instead of migrating this data to the new systems.

In any case, in chapter 17, I will explore AI, and I can envision improvements in these efforts given the advancements occurring in AI technology.

However, depending on the systems in place and the penetration of new techniques such as AI within the solution sets, there is a good chance that the discussion here will still be considered relevant and represents an opportunity for improved strategic execution and the reduction of timelines when it comes to data migration.

PART VI

Dynamic Execution

Summary And Emerging Technologies

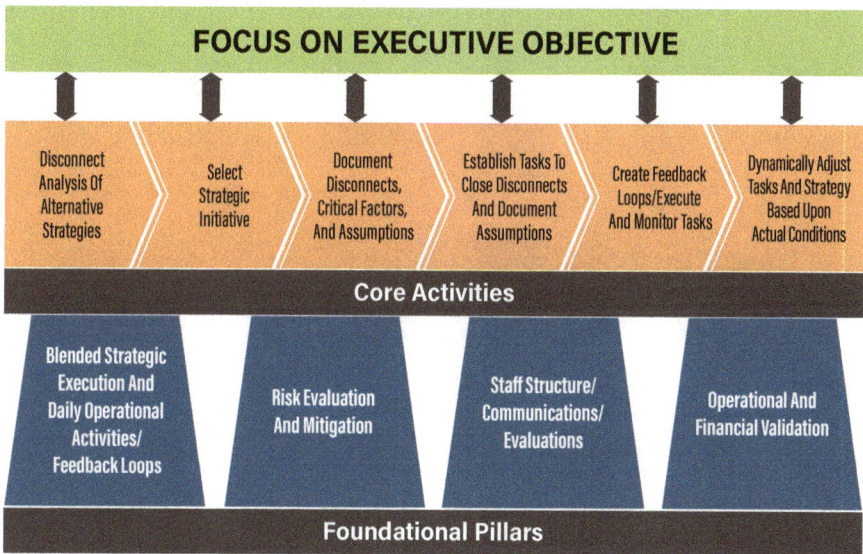

FOCUS ON EXECUTIVE OBJECTIVE

| Disconnect Analysis Of Alternative Strategies | Select Strategic Initiative | Document Disconnects, Critical Factors, And Assumptions | Establish Tasks To Close Disconnects And Document Assumptions | Create Feedback Loops/Execute And Monitor Tasks | Dynamically Adjust Tasks And Strategy Based Upon Actual Conditions |

Core Activities

| Blended Strategic Execution And Daily Operational Activities/ Feedback Loops | Risk Evaluation And Mitigation | Staff Structure/ Communications/ Evaluations | Operational And Financial Validation |

Foundational Pillars

Chapters 16 and 17 conclude with a final review of how Dynamic Execution provides today's C-suite with a new dynamic framework for the accomplishment of critical objectives using innovative concepts, tools, and techniques.

I explore how Dynamic Execution goes beyond traditional executive dashboards and conclude with a discussion of Dynamic Execution in today's world of artificial intelligence (AI) and emerging technologies.

16

Beyond Dashboards

Illustration: Early in my career as a junior executive, I pushed to upgrade our manufacturing and financial software.

I did my homework and found a major vendor with a software solution that had a large user base and all the functionality I thought we needed. It was a tough internal sell since the COO had to postpone the acquisition of some major equipment in order to support my necessary budget.

We acquired the system and bought into the use of the vendor's experts along with their implementation plan and services.

We did everything right and were told it would be a twelve-month project.

Initially, everything went as planned, and my reports to executive management were positive.

Unfortunately, nine months into the project, the wheels came off.

While we were able to properly configure and prepare to launch the manufacturing functionality, we discovered it did not work in the type of environment we were operating in.

The experts told us that the only fix for the issue would be to incur the cost of customizing the software and significantly extend the execution timeline.

When I discussed with the experts how to present these newfound issues to executive management, the recommendation I received was that "they should understand since this is not uncommon when implementing such a major software initiative. Therefore, as senior management, if they are truly committed to the project, they need to just understand and move forward."

To this day, I can remember my response to the experts.

"If you think that I am going to tell executive management, who committed significant company resources to this project and spent substantial amounts of money for the purchase of what is supposed to be the best software solution, implementation methodology, and experts, that a failure of the project would be the result of a lack of their understanding and commitment, you are out of your mind."

Fortunately, I took the time to perform what I would come to call a disconnect analysis and discovered that we could reconfigure the system without any major programming and solve the challenges.

This allowed me to avoid having a ridiculous conversation with executive management.

Instead, I was able to point out to them that while the project would be slightly delayed, we were able to obtain the required functionality in our environment even though the software really was not structured to handle our type of conditions.

Obviously, in retrospect, if we had been using Dynamic Execution and performed a proper front-end disconnect analysis, we could have determined the issue ahead of time and avoided the challenges.

I cannot even count the number of times over the years I was in meetings where a strategic initiative was having these sorts of challenges, and the C-suite was asking tough questions.

While I could fill pages here with legitimate answers, inaccurate answers, clueless answers, justifications, apologies, and just plain excuses that were given, including by myself, I won't.

Instead, I will explain that Dynamic Execution and the other concepts, tools, and methodologies discussed in this book provide the capability and a structure to not only quickly answer tough questions but actually avoid the need to ask them in the first place.

It was through the struggles and challenges I personally had on both the executive side asking these sorts of questions and as the person responsible for trying to answer these sorts of questions that I realized there had to be a better way.

I discovered the hard way that, even using the most sophisticated of available project management tools and implementation methodologies and the most talented experts, the ability to obtain strategic initiative execution that accomplished the required objectives on time, at budget, and with full functionality was filled with challenges and significant exposure to failure.

While in many applications the use of dashboards can represent a useful tool, executive monitoring and control of strategic initiative executions is not one of them. Nor are the occasional project update meetings reviewing the implementation and budget status under varying presentation and review structures, content, and executive time commitments.

However, Dynamic Execution has built-in capability for executives to easily understand, monitor, and control, from the beginning to the end, the successful execution of an objective and its associated strategic initiatives.

Built-In Information Platform

Under Dynamic Execution, the goal is to provide executives with an information platform that, in a time-efficient context, provides easy-to-understand data for all of the dynamics, critical factors, and exposures associated with the execution of a strategy that is expected to successfully result in the established objective.

First, Dynamic Execution incorporates built-in exposure analysis that goes well beyond the typical traditional functionality analysis used in the selection of a strategic initiative.

The exposure analysis used in the selection of the strategy results in a comprehensive and clear documentation of:

- Disconnects, critical factors, and assumptions
- Functionality trade-offs and "when not if" considerations
- Potential risk factors
- Cash and budget considerations
- Financial validation of expected results

This documentation provides a straightforward, understandable overview and analysis of the complexity, challenges, and effort required to execute the strategic initiative successfully.

No matter how good the functionality derived from a selected strategy might appear at meeting the goals of an objective, it is this information that provides a true reflection of the reality of what it will take to execute the strategy. This information provides executive management and the rest of the organization with an extremely powerful tool to pragmatically assess what it will really take to execute the strategy and, therefore, the real likelihood of success.

From an executive perspective, reviewing this documentation is a time-efficient, straightforward approach to understanding and questioning the thought process and dynamics associated with a selected strategy.

Given that this level of analysis should be performed for each individual alternative strategy under consideration, it also provides executives the capability to quickly determine and potentially challenge the *whys* behind the final selection.

Built-In Monitoring And Control

Under Dynamic Execution, the goal is to provide executives with a time-efficient, built-in system for monitoring and controlling actual conditions versus critical factors and assumptions.

This allows executives to immediately recognize, assess, and address exposures during the strategic execution.

A major component of Dynamic Execution is the continuous monitoring, analysis, and feedback of actual conditions to strategy, disconnects, assumption criteria, and risk.

For each task and the overall selected strategy, there is documentation of the specific conditions, critical requirements, and assumptions for monitoring and feedback criteria. These criteria are then used to establish monitoring integration points within the operational feedback-loop structure.

Feedback loops support the timely and immediate bidirectional communication for the monitoring, analysis, financial validation, and adjustments required during the initiative's execution.

When monitoring actual conditions against feedback criteria indicates a potential issue, this information is immediately communicated for analysis, including a possible financial revalidation.

This analysis can result in various alternative actions, including the possible modification of tasks and/or the selected strategy.

From both an executive and organizational perspective, the obvious benefits of this built-in monitoring and control structure are the immediate availability of the status, issues, and challenges associated with strategic/objective execution.

In addition, the information and analysis are based upon actual quantifiable data that can be easily and directly traced back to the critical criteria, assumptions, risks, and analysis used during the selection of the strategy.

This provides executives with an ability to continuously and efficiently monitor and understand the status and dynamics of a strategic/objective execution based upon credible information.

Built-In Expanded Execution Capabilities

Under Dynamic Execution, the goal is to provide executives with a built-in capability to increase the availability of strategic execution capacity through reduced execution timelines, blended strategic and operational activities, and dynamic scheduling.

The dynamic aspect of Dynamic Execution inherently supports a built-in capability to reduce the timelines associated with strategic executions.

From advance critical-factor/assumption testing to the laser focus on actual disconnects to the power of assumption monitoring and feedback loops, there exists the opportunity to eliminate avoidable time requirements.

A blended environment of continuously executing strategic initiative activities with day-to-day operational activities also intrinsically represents the significant benefit of constantly available strategic execution capacity.

In addition, this blended environment supports dynamic scheduling and staff empowerment, which infuses major efficiency into the execution process.

There are two major benefits derived from these efficiencies and reduced timelines.

First, the shorter the timeline, the less potential there is for failure due to perpetually changing conditions.

Second, shorter timelines not only provide the capacity to execute more initiatives in the same period of time, but also increase the ability to manage and execute multiple initiatives simultaneously.

This, in turn, has the benefit of creating an ability to better manage "when not if" challenges.

Built-In Objective Management Control And Oversight Capabilities

Dynamic Execution represents a fully integrated closed-loop structure that systematically builds and documents the critical information and data necessary for the selection and execution of strategies for the accomplishment of executive objectives.

From the documentation of the critical information associated with the development of the objectives, through the analytical information utilized in the selection of strategies, to the data required for the actual execution and monitoring of the selected strategies, Dynamic Execution builds a platform of information and data that provides a quick, efficient, and effective executive capability for the understanding, oversight, and control of all the dynamics related to the accomplishment of their objectives.

The structure and data of the resource-to-disconnect analysis represent a single, comprehensive, integrated, and closed-loop capability that the executives and organization can use to immediately assess the status, demands, requirements, and dynamics of the strategic/objective executions at any point in time.

This real-time information and analytical capability allow the executive to maintain objective management involvement and oversight in a comprehensive, straightforward, and time-efficient context.

Summary

I hope it is obvious that these built-in capabilities represent a new set of opportunities for improved executive strategic and objective execution management, control, and involvement—involvement that is both effective and time efficient in providing the ultimate value of significantly increasing the accomplishment of the organizational objectives.

Dynamic Execution represents the ability for executives to obtain true objective management.

Dynamic Execution also finally provides executives with the ability to effectively fight their major enemy: time.

17

Dynamic Execution And Artificial Intelligence (AI)/ Emerging Technologies

I must admit up front that I cannot consider myself a profound expert in AI.

However, I do have a significant amount of experience over the years in the understanding and application of major technological advancements, including AI.

I have been fortunate that I have been able to explore applications and had firsthand access to some leading-edge technologies, including one of the first voice recognition boards, analog to digital video capture technology, early internet merchant processing systems, and I even oversaw the launch of an early telematics offering.

Regarding AI, early in my career, both at the executive and at the execution level, I was involved with IBM and others trying to determine possible opportunities for the use of emerging AI technology.

In this chapter, I intended to provide some firsthand AI experiences and discuss the use of Dynamic Execution in the execution of AI opportunities.

However, before I do that, I want to establish a framework for AI that will represent a context I can use during my discussion.

AI Framework For Discussion

I know there are all sorts of technical definitions and concepts associated with AI, but here, from an executive viewpoint, I want to focus on AI from a more simplified applications perspective. Therefore, I might not always be perfectly consistent or accurate with hardcore terminology and concepts, but from an applications overview perspective, I think it will still all make sense.

From an applications perspective, I like to view AI as providing a spectrum of application capabilities.

Operational AI Tools

The first set of applications is really a new generation of tools that, if integrated into an organization's operations, can improve operating efficiencies. These, more often than not, represent applications that can be utilized across a broad base of users. I include in this category applications like chatbots, conversational AI, digital assistants, and GPS. These applications require access to large databases of information from which to learn and quickly formulate output.

Diagnostic/Analytical AI

These AI applications focus on the ability to quickly analyze a set of conditions as they relate to a known set of information that in turn allows them to predict what exists based upon that information.

These systems continue to learn because the database of information the application uses in its analytics is continuously increasing from new experiences, thereby making the predictions potentially more and more accurate.

Illustration: Back in the late 1980s and early 1990s, I was involved with an executive objective to try to mitigate a major financial risk.

The organization provided customers with fixed-priced contracts for a material-intensive product where the material was purchased as a commodity but had continuously fluctuating prices and no futures market. Therefore, no natural commodity-hedging vehicles existed.

These were significantly large customer contracts so there was no ability to cover this exposure through the current purchasing and inventorying of materials at the cost associated with the quoted pricing. The sheer magnitude of the required inventory that would need to be acquired was financially impossible.

Being the techno-geek I was, at the time I had a lot of interaction with people in the world of emerging technology including AI and I was introduced to a professor with expertise in commodities and cross-hedging.

Between this expertise and his access to state-of-the-art computing and data resource capabilities, along with weeks of high-powered computer processing time, the existence of a cross hedge for our commodity was determined. We found two traded commodities that represented this cross hedge.

We immediately leveraged this cross-hedging opportunity, thereby, over time, mitigating a significant amount of risk.

More importantly, the more often the cross-hedging programs were executed, the additional information available from the prior iterations improved the accuracy of the newly executed cross hedges.

This was revolutionary at the time and was only possible because of the relationship that was established with that professor and major university that had state-of-the-art computing capability, sufficient capacity, and access to major amounts of required data.

Fast forwarding to today, I would include the AI applications being developed and utilized in medical diagnoses, biotech, and smart manufacturing within this category.

Machine Learning AI

These AI applications have a true ability to learn and make decisions without human interaction. In my context, these applications, from the very initial start, begin learning through actual experiences, thereby continually improving their output's sophistication and accomplishment.

Illustration: Once again, back in the late 1980s and early 1990s, I saw the opportunity to use AI to greatly improve the efficiency of cutting leather for the automotive industry.

This was a very complex task in that an automotive seat of finished leather is composed of multiple sizes and shapes of cut out leather patterns all sewn together. Each of these patterns had a unique cutting die that an individual would place on a finished hide of leather. All these dies would then be punched out into the final pieces of cut patterns.

Of course, the efficiency/profitability of this operation was highly dependent on placing all of these various dies/patterns on the hide in a configuration that minimized the scrap generated from the off-fall between the dies.

Unfortunately, unlike fabric or vinyl, which came on a roll in a consistent size and pattern, this process was made even more complex in that every hide was unique in its size, shape, and defects (such as holes or scratches).

Before the cutters were even able to determine the best layout of the dies, they had to mark the location of the defects. That way they could cut around them and not have defects appear in the finished cut out.

Cutters could then start to conceptualize what dies should be placed where based upon the actual shape, size, and defects of the hide they were dealing with.

To this day I think the individuals performing this layout of patterns were some of the most impressive people I have worked with. They possessed an unbelievable skill set and ability to geometrically envision where to place all of these varying patterns across a continuously changing background of hides.

In any case, this is where I saw a possible opportunity for the use of artificial intelligence.

Working with a university and other experts, it was believed that both scanning technology and optimization algorithms were available to attempt to improve the maximization of the layout of these cut patterns, thereby minimizing the scrap.

The process would look like the following. First, place the hide on a table and manually mark the defects. Note, it was anticipated that over time even the determination of the defects could eventually be learned (a form of AI) and used through the scanning of the hide by the computer to establish the type and location of the defects.

Next, use the scanned hide and a known set of cutting pattern shapes to run a maximization model that would project with light the placement of the patterns on the hide with the objective of minimizing scrap. Finally, place the patterns based on the computer projection and punch the dies into their final patterns.

Unfortunately, given that each hide was unique, while the process was determined to be achievable, the amount of time to process the maximization model was too long to make it economically feasible.

However, before we gave up, I wanted to try to use AI in a new way to solve this challenge by not running the optimization model from start to conclusion for each and every single hide.

Instead, I felt we needed to limit the optimization modeling on any given hide to a specific number of iterations.

While we would not necessarily maximize the layout of the patterns for that specific hide, we could use the information to have the computer learn over time, thereby improving its layout as it continued to process future hides.

In other words, the computer would learn over time by continually building a database of initial hide shape, size, and defect configurations, along with the last arrangement of patterns used on that hide configuration. Instead of the algorithm starting from ground zero for each hide, it would first scan the new hide and search the existing database of cut hides to find a hide that had the closest match to the size, shape, and defect patterns of the hide being scanned.

The computer could then start the optimization model using the last pattern arrangement that existed for the hide selected from the database. This meant that as time went on, the computer automatically continued to learn through the accumulated database of pattern arrangements to hide configurations and would become more and more knowledgeable/ efficient in minimizing scrap—could be considered machine learning AI at its finest.

Regrettably, while the concepts and applications were proven to be viable, the computing power and database technology did not exist back then to support a financially feasible result.

Today's Executives

Today's executives find themselves in an environment where advancements in technology have provided an ability to create, store, and maintain massive databases of various types of information along with significant advancements in computing power.

This is neither good nor bad. Exciting is probably the best word to describe it.

However, when these conditions are wrapped in an intensive state of promotional, economical, and media overload, it begs the question, as executives, how should we proceed and how rapidly should we proceed?

As executives, the answer to these questions is to approach AI (together with all emerging technologies) with a laser focus on applications and objectives.

I started the AI discussion by first defining AI from an applications perspective for several reasons.

From an executive's perspective, and consistent with Dynamic Execution, the focus should be on objective management.

Therefore, the focus should be on what AI applications exist that have the potential to positively assist in the accomplishment of defined executive/organizational objectives.

If there are potential AI applications that should be considered, executives should follow Dynamic Execution starting with asking (a) what are the disconnects (including functionality trade-offs) between the organization's existing conditions and the requirements of the AI application, (b) how much effort and cost will be incurred to close these disconnects, (c) what other risks exist, and (d) have the assumptions and expectations been operationally and financially validated. Bottom line, AI should be approached like any other technology and therefore, examined and executed consistent with using Dynamic Execution that has a focus on the accomplishment of critical objectives.

As indicated in my personal illustrations above, the concepts associated with AI are not as new as some might be led to believe.

Again, what has changed is the evolution to having massive databases of various types of information and a significant advancement in computing power.

However, this evolution and advancement in these technologies also represent their own set of conditions, requirements, and dynamics.

For example, confidentiality, reliability, quality of output, cost, and required technology are all new dynamics associated with AI.

Therefore, consistent with Dynamic Execution, executives need to examine these new external and internal AI conditions and dynamics from a perspective of change drivers, opportunities, and risks.

Change should be equated to specific objectives with alternative strategies that can be properly evaluated.

The concept of "when not if" tells us that we are beyond the point of whether artificial intelligence will affect our organizations. So, our focus should be on the "when" and in what context (the *why*).

The reality today is that for most individuals and organizations, the costs associated with AI are too great to allow for major self-developed capabilities.

AI still requires the accumulation of or access to massive amounts of data and computing power to work.

This means that only the government and the largest organizations are currently in the best positions to directly participate as borne out by the initiatives at Amazon, UPS, Google, and other large organizations.

It also means that for most, utilization of AI will be limited to operational AI tool applications discussed above that are available in the marketplace.

If similar to my attempts in the 1990s, an organization decides there might be an internal AI opportunity, then I will once again tell you to use Dynamic Execution, including disconnect analysis, as a tool to assist in the evaluation.

Finally, functionality trade-off analysis is a powerful tool to use when it is determined that there might be benefit in the utilization of an AI application.

A functionality trade-off exists when the selection of one functionality (i.e., an external AI application) is interconnected in such a way that you cannot obtain that functionality without sacrificing another desired functionality or capability. In this case, this generally represents some sort of risk to the organization.

Some of the biggest potential functionality risks that have already been associated with existing AI applications include inaccuracy of output because the underlying external data in the AI database is overly summarized, biased, incomplete, or not inclusive of the data required to provide an accurate result relative to your conditions.

There is also an AI requirement to provide user data that is personal, confidential, or broader than necessary thereby opening your organization to new security, data usage, or other risks.

There is a reliance on future ongoing access to external AI functionality versus internal functionality and that data integrity will be maintained in the future. This risk can be significant depending on the level of dependence and significance the AI functionality represents to your organization.

Since this is an external versus internal functionality, there can be known or unknown modifications and updates to the AI functionality or database that invalidate or negatively affect the utilization of the output from the AI application.

Again, AI needs to be addressed in the same Dynamic Execution context as any other emerging technology we have been exposed to in the past.

As executives, you should not be reactionary but analytical.

By employing Dynamic Execution, AI needs to be continuously monitored for existing or emerging opportunities and then carefully analyzed from a disconnect, risk, functionality trade-off, and "when not if" perspective.

Acknowledgments

To the hundreds of people who over the years have mentored, taught, collaborated with, and supported me. Most of all, my wife Nancy and our seven children, who truly represent the real definition of an understanding and supportive family.

A special thanks to Pamela Roberts for all of her assistance.

About The Author

Tom Somodi is an executive, entrepreneur, and innovator. He is an author, speaker, and consultant on the subject of change. His extensive business experience includes taking a company public during the difficult financial markets of 2011 that provided a nine-times return and a market capitalization approaching 900 million dollars within three years to initial investors. His executive management-level experience includes domestic and international startups, mergers and acquisitions, reorganizations, and strategic change initiatives in technology, manufacturing, distribution, and service organizations. His international experience encompasses China/Asia, UK/Europe, South Africa, Mexico, Canada, and the Caribbean. Tom has been a certified public accountant and has significant public and private sector executive and board-level experience, including positions as chief executive officer, chief operating officer, chief financial officer, and chief strategy officer.

Tom is the author of the reference book, *The Science Of Change: Basics Behind Why Change Succeeds And Fails.*

List of Figures

Works Cited

1   Andrea Belk Olson, "4 Common Reasons Strategies Fail," *Harvard Business Review*, June 24, 2022, https://hbr.org/2022/06/4-common-reasons-strategies-fail and Michael Bucy, Bill Schaninger, Kate VanAkin, and Brooke Weddle, "Losing from day one: Why even successful transformations fall short," *McKinsey & Company*, December 7, 2021, https://www.mckinsey.com/capabilities/people-and-organizational-performance/our-insights/successful-transformations.

2   Denise Dahlhoff, "Why Target's Canadian Expansion Failed, *Harvard Business Review*, January 20, 2015, https://hbr.org/2015/01/why-targets-canadian-expansion-failed.

3   Olson, "4 Common Reasons," and Bucy et al., "Losing from day one."

4   Jason Stein, "Automotive Legends and Heroes: W. Edwards Deming," *East Valley Tribune*, June 8, 2008, Updated October 7, 2011, https://www.eastvalleytribune.com/money/automotive-legends-and-heroes-w-edwards-deming/article_027c8271-7cd2-5049-b15f-56ee7026f8bc.html.

5   Dahlhoff, "Why Target's Canadian Expansion Failed."

6   Olson, "4 Common Reasons," and Bucy et al., "Losing from day one."

7   *The Food that Built America*, season 4, episode 1, "Breakfast that Pops," directed by Drew Painter, written by Shari Ortner, Brian Burstein, and Harry Courniotes, aired February 19, 2023, on The HISTORY Channel.

8   Kimberly Amadeo, "Historical US Unemployment Rate by Year," *The Balance Money*, Updated on December 6, 2022, https://www.thebalancemoney.com/unemployment-rate-by-year-3305506#citation-20.

9   John Kander and Fred Ebb, "Money," In *Cabaret*, Viking Press, 1966.

Index

www.ingramcontent.com/pod-product-compliance
Lightning Source LLC
Chambersburg PA
CBHW070303200326
41518CB00010B/1871